BIBLICAL CHRISTIAN MARRIAGE

BIBLICAL CHRISTIAN MARRIAGE

Cliff Edwards

JOHN KNOX PRESS
ATLANTA

Library of Congress Cataloging in Publication Data

Edward, Cliff, 1931-
  Biblical Christian marriage.

  1. Marriage. I. Title.
BV835.E35   248'.4   76-44973
ISBN 0-8042-1100-0

© copyright 1977 John Knox Press
Printed in the United States of America
Atlanta, Georgia

For *Ted and Louise Snyder,*
who have meant so much to me.

For *Dr. Henlee H. Barnette,*
a man of moral courage and an inpsiration to many.

CONTENTS

INTRODUCTION

Almost two thousand years ago the Apostle Paul stated frankly that "those who marry will have worldly troubles, and I would spare you that." (1 Cor. 7:28 R.S.V.) But centuries before Paul, the author of the book of Job stated that human beings are "born to trouble as the sparks fly upward." (Job 5:7 R.S.V.) While this does not mean that human life is nothing but one trouble after another, it should help to set things in better perspective. Christians should not think that they are weird or perverse if in marriage they experience troubles and crises. Such is to be expected.

Marriage today in the Western world is encountering more threats and disrupting influences than it has faced in many generations. And yet the conviction that marriage is a meaningful commitment has never been stronger. More than their words, the actual behavior of people tells us that very large numbers of people still regard marriage as a significant and vital option. Even the majority of those Americans who divorce will eventually marry again. They are far from renouncing marriage itself as a lost cause.

There is no need to try to convince millions of people of the values of marriage, for they are already convinced. Nor is there any point in perpetually telling most of them to love each other and to show goodwill toward each other, for they know already that they should do this. But marriages are not held together by love and goodwill alone. The time has come for couples to seek out some new and better resources that will help them in their marital commitment. Stoicism might lead a married couple to imagine that together they possess in themselves all the basic resources for sustaining a meaningful marriage. But Christian teaching makes it clear that as finite creatures, they are at every moment dependent on all sorts of external resources. There is no shame in recognizing this fact. It is an elementary point of common sense and necessary worldly wisdom.

Stoicism forgets that marriages do not thrive without some favorable external resources and conditions. Without these conditions, a couple may still live together in the same house and engage in certain marital rituals, but marriage as a vital and meaningful relationship will not be a likelihood for them. Fish are not profoundly aware of just how dependent they are on the water they live and move in. Similarly, we sometimes forget that human beings depend on a rich and complex environment that is both physical and social in nature. In addition to requiring the normal supply of oxygen, food, and other physical and social stimuli, a hardy marriage requires very special social stimuli and supports. It requires a large degree of practical know-how if it is to remain a robust and enriching relationship.

Today marriage must cope with drastic and sweeping changes within the social environment, changes that have been building up steadily since the First World War. There are real things out there in the social and material environment which did not exist even sixty or seventy years ago. But if new external threats exist, there exist also new, powerful, and interesting things which can *strengthen* the marital commitment. For example, today in Christian seminaries and schools, a number of future ministers and church workers are receiving practical training specifically in marriage and family counseling. This particular social process of training Christians in marital counseling did not exist thirty years ago except in very rare cases. A number of skilled ministers have become very important resources which husbands and wives sometimes turn to as a concrete means of keeping their marriage alive and secure.

My persistent plan has been to make this book a practical handbook for those people who are willing to fight for the right to a meaningful Christian marriage. Because there are external forces that are destroying marriages every day, married couples need to be equipped for handling the threats and challenges to their marriage.

The general framework from which I have written this book is evangelical Christianity, and the major working assumption is that this framework has more resources and options than many Christians themselves have ever dreamed possible. At the same time, another working assumption is that Christians can and must find practical insight and information from whatever source they can. There is nothing in the faith which teaches that the evangelical approach alone is the source of all light and illumination which the Creator has bestowed upon the human race.

It is encouraging to see that very recently some Christians, while contending that they are not *of* the world, nevertheless are remembering that they are most definitely *in* the world. It is here in this world that they have for now the responsibility to carry out their lives, whether married or single. Christ said that there will be no marriages in heaven, which makes marriage a strictly earthly venture. What I have written in the following pages is for very finite and earthly human beings who are married and who have to maintain their marriage by employing a good deal of worldly wisdom. Jesus enjoined his disciples to be not just as harmless as doves, but also wise as serpents.

In the book, two chapters—the one on abortion and the one on divorce—will probably be very controversial for some of my readers. But I did not want this book to be pablum. Marriage and family life have some very tough, crucial, and critical decisions that demand to be faced now.

Throughout all the chapters, I have drawn heavily from two sources in addition to Christianity. They are behaviorism and cognitivism. Very briefly, the former emphasizes the importance of getting strength and support from the multi-layered environment. The latter emphasizes the point that what people believe often affects what they do and how they feel. Married couples can appropriate some of the techniques of behaviorism in order to strengthen themselves against powerful external threats. Cognitivism will be important in this book because I will examine some of the more practically important conceptions and misconceptions of marriage.

I

WHEN CHRISTIANS BECOME DEPRESSED

The Universality of Depression

You may be asking, "Why should a book on marriage include a chapter on depression?" My answer is two-fold. First, in some cases a marriage relationship can be seriously threatened by certain kinds and intensities of depression. Second, sometimes the interaction between husband and wife becomes so frustrating that it brings about depression for at least one of them. Fortunately the period of the emotional "low" can often be restricted in such a way as to prevent it from spreading throughout the entire marriage.

It is normal for most people to expect some depression, and there is no point in worrying over the fact that they may now and then feel moderately depressed. My concern in this chapter is to deal with serious depression when it is either a symptom of destructive marital conflict or a cause of heavy gloom and guilt affecting both husband and wife, or even affecting the children in many cases.

I have chosen to place this chapter on depression at the front of the book for one basic reason. The tactics and tools developed in this chapter will be quite useful to you throughout the remainder of the book.

Depression is a universal phenomenon which strikes in degrees of severity! A careful reading of the Bible shows that Job and King Saul were not the only ones to suffer from this malady. Elijah, Hannah, Habakkuk, Ezekiel, Jeremiah, and a few of the writers of the Psalms experienced it, some of them more severely than others. A number of the early Christians seemed to become depressed as time went on and the second coming of Christ failed to materialize as expected.[1] Church history is filled with accounts of Christian men and women who at different periods in their lives became deeply disturbed, some to the point of severe withdrawal.

Two noted non-Christians—Bertrand Russell and Sigmund Freud—knew personally what it was to be depressed. During two periods of his life, Russell thought seriously of suicide. But he changed his mind and lived on into his late nineties. Freud, who also lived to be an old man, suffered considerable pain during the last sixteen years of his life. Curious as it seems, his period of depression came when he was only thirty-eight years old. His work was impeded during that time when he was afflicted with obsessive thoughts of how long he still had to live after having suffered some "questionably anginal attacks."[2] Either the thought of one's own death or the actual experience of seeing one's close friend or family member die can bring about depression.

The Case of Anna Young*

There are many causes and conditions of depression. But what exactly is depression? It is found in varying degrees of severity. The most severe form is a state of abject hopelessness, loss of interest in most things, disengagement from activities and involvements, and extreme apathy. I have not mentioned the *feelings* that accompany this withdrawal behavior. Sometimes depression takes place even when the agent does not feel it, because he has disconnected himself from certain feelings.

*Unless clearly stated otherwise, the names of individuals appearing as case studies in this book have been changed to respect the individuals' rights of privacy. All case studies are actual. In some cases, slight changes have been made in order to prevent identification.

Depression may be described as a process in which the individual is slowly being cut off from sources of life. It is easy to understand that without food and drink, we will die; and some people in depression come close to giving up these essentials. But sometimes we forget that we take in also all sorts of *social* nourishment. The friendly words, smiles, comments about our work or clothes, conversation about our children and projects and interests, etc.—these are all vital input stimulating our brains and bodies, and strengthening us in countless ways.

Anna Young, a very bright woman in her early forties, was missed at church a few Sundays. One of the members called to learn what was wrong. Her husband, Mel, answered. Anna would not talk to the caller even though the two of them were good friends. Mel explained on the phone that Anna had quit her job, had drawn the curtains in the house, and was refusing to leave the house. Always a very conscientious person, Anna no longer cared about her appearance and was uninterested in seeing anyone. Always a reader and intelligent conversationist about what she was reading, Anna no longer cared to read. Such extreme withdrawal *is* severe depression. Accompanying her withdrawal behavior were also feelings—guilt, shame, bewilderment, etc. She even attempted suicide, but the way she went about it revealed that she was not yet willing to close the lid to her own casket. She was hopeless and helpless, yet not to the point of demanding that her husband get out of the house. It is difficult to know the dynamics that go on between any husband and wife, but Mel did not give up even though many men in his situation would have. After trying a number of things to no avail, he sent his wife to live with a psychologist in another town because the psychologist —a woman—had been Anna's good friend for a long time. Mel had earlier thought of shock therapy, but he could not bring himself to do this to his wife. Unfortunately, the psychologist friend could not help Anna.

I am happy to report that today Anna, back at work, is cheerful and as bright and keen as ever — only now she has a certain wisdom which has given her greater emotional depth. What happened to bring about this astounding recovery? The psychologist friend, realizing that she could not turn the tide of Anna's depression, nevertheless managed to keep her alive and to refer her to a very special psychiatrist in a mental health clinic. After six weeks of working with the psychiatrist and two psychologists in the clinic, and receiving antidepressant drug therapy, Anna came home. The change in the woman is absolutely remarkable.

A number of things brought about Anna's severe depression. Paradoxically, she had failed to learn the skill of withdrawing from *certain* harmful cues and signals in her environment. Unable to turn off or ignore these harmful signals, she became so swamped and flooded by them that she had to withdraw from *almost all* signals. In short, she was on the verge of drowning in the duties and responsibilities that she had allowed to develop in her life indiscriminately and without careful evaluation.

Psychologist O. Hobart Mowrer says that most emotional disturbance is really a form of *irresponsibility*. There is some truth in this assertion if we define irresponsibility as the failure to *respond* (to be responsive) to the signals and cues that are our duties. But what Mowrer fails to explore in his book *The Crisis in Psychiatry and Religion*[3] is how it is that people become irresponsible or unresponsive to their duties. In Anna's particular case, she simply had *too many conflicting signals,* too many mixed-up cues to respond to. The conflict inside was a mere reflection of (or response to) the conflicting signals *outside*—in her job and in her expectations as a parent.

Anna's case is simply a more intensified version of a large number of people's cases. No normal human being could have survived Anna's situation. The job that she had before her severe depression came about has now been changed. Anna did not change jobs; rather those with whom she worked finally came to see that *the job itself had to be changed.*

This is an appropriate place to introduce some of the practical procedures of behaviorism and behavioral therapy, which has in recent years proved to be quite successful in dealing with some of the personal problems of individuals. The noted psychologist, Dr. Wayne Oates, expressing appreciation for "the great contributions that the behavioral psychologists have made to religious life and practice," notes that "behavioral therapy is a kind . . . that can be learned in the simplest form by lay persons."[4]

Observing Your Responses, Signals, and Reinforcers

Behaviorism gets its name from the fact that it emphasizes human *behavior* as the unit of study. Human behavior is a complex repertoire of responses. The word "response" is a key term, for human beings are evaluated according to whether they are *respons*ive and *respons*ible. To be totally unrespons*ive* is to be dead as an individual. To be totally irrespons*ible* is to be dead socially and morally. In its extreme state, depression is severe unresponsiveness.

The significance of behaviorism lies in its insistence that responses are always in connection with something else that brings out the responses. Hence, in order to gain some control of their responses, people have to have some knowledge of *what* it is in their physical and social environment that they are responding *to*. After all, people do not respond or act in a vacuum.

According to modern behaviorism, the human individual is not simply a set of reflexes. Rather, the individual is involved with his environment and has an impact on it; that is, he operates on it. By the same token, the environment has an impact back on the individual. When Johnny gives his girlfriend half his popsicle, she in turn will under normal conditions smile or show appreciation. Her smile is a *positive reinforcer* because it supports or strengthens Johnny's unselfish act. To reinforce or strengthen an act is to increase the likelihood that the same sort of act will reoccur on a later occasion.

However, if Johnny hits a wasps' nest and gets stung, he will find the sting to be *punishment* rather than positive reinforcement. Ordinarily, when punishment follows an act or response, then that response is *less* likely to be repeated.

There is nothing especially mysterious about this interaction between responses and the reward or punishment that follows. Behaviorism simply builds upon this elementary principle of interaction; it builds by making very detailed observations and by

keeping accurate records of the patterns that develop between responses and their rewards and punishments.

There is another crucial element, namely, the *signal or cue*
that comes on the scene *before* the response is released. So what
we have is a sequence of (1) signal, (2) response, and (3) reward
or punishment. Fortunately, the signal in our environment has
two arrows, so to speak. One leads to the response and the other
leads to the reward or punishment. For example, the sight of the
wasps' nest serves as a signal to an active and curious boy like
Johnny. First, the signal moves Johnny to respond by hitting the
nest. But, fortunately, the signal, in the second place, points to
the *previous punishment* that came when Johnny responded by hitting the nest. I will not go into the details of how signals function in this two-fold way. Rather, the point here is that people
live their lives in response to signals and in light of the consequences that follow their responses.

This interplay of signals, responses, and consequences (rewards and punishments) is what behavioral therapy devotes itself
to keeping track of in the lives of individuals. People develop
"problems" when the same set of responses leads to both reward
and punishment, as in the case of Anna Young. The signals,
therefore, are in conflict because they "lead to" consequences
that clash with one another.

The Confusion of Signals and Clash of Consequences

Imagine yourself driving through a town where in one block
the green light is a clear signal to drive on, whereas in the next
block the green light "means" that if you fail to stop your car,
you will be pulled over by a traffic cop and given a ticket. Then
on the following day all the stop signs mean "proceed ahead,"
while the 30 M.P.H. sign means "stop." Well, if given a few
more conflicting signals of this sort, you will very likely try to
avoid this weird town altogether. Now, if you could not go
around this town but had to go through it, what would you do if
the traffic director each month erected more traffic signals with

mixed-up meanings, that is, with clashing consequences? In this confusing mess, what would give a reward in one block on one day would give punishment on another day—and so on and on with no reliable and predictable pattern.

After a few days of this confusion, you would simply stay at home; or if caught in the middle of a traffic jam in this town, you might simply stop and slump down in the floor of your car because you had "had it" with the crazy town and its traffic director. In fact, once when I was in the mixed-up Boston traffic, back in the late 1950s, I observed a frustrated driver who suddenly had "had it." In the middle of the traffic he stopped his car, got out, and with briefcase in hand walked to work.

Anna Young's job was very much like this crazy imaginary town that I referred to above. Anna was quite sane, but the signals and consequences of the job were crazy. Unfortunately, because of her excessively rigid background, she could not bring herself simply to quit the stupid job or even to go to the equivalent of the traffic director of the job. Instead, she tried to respond in a responsible manner to the mixed-up signals until she could no longer endure it. She finally withdrew—from practically everything—and blamed herself for not being able to handle the job. Apparently, most of her world of signals and consequences flooded her, and she was unable to swim in the flood any longer. She came very close to drowning.

To make this story short, Anna's boss eventually got the message and turned off the flood of impossible signals. That is, when Anna went back to work, the signals that used to stimulate her were reorganized and made more orderly and fewer than they had been before her withdrawal. Working at Anna's job as it used to be may be compared to drinking from a fire hose that is going full blast. It is no wonder that Anna was knocked flat.

She had to learn the hard way that there are lots of crazy signals in the world and that she is not duty-bound to respond to them all. Because it was on her job that the confusing signals were given to her, Anna felt that she was morally obligated to respond to them. Fortunately, she eventually was able to come to terms with her own finitude and to see that all human responsibility is limited. By learning to become *insensitive to certain crazy signals,* Anna was thus freed to become more sensitive and responsive to signals leading to enjoyable and responsible consequences.

The Model

In recent years behavioral therapists have come to see how important "modeling" is in human learning. A person does not always have to experience directly the consequences of a response. He or she can observe the transaction in *other* people. If Elizabeth can see that Sherry is rewarded in responding to certain signals, she can also copy Sherry's behavior in the hope of receiving a similar reward. A school teacher once explained to me how a new child in her class was "cured" of creating disturbances. After ignoring this student and refusing to reward him for being a distraction to the class members at work, the teacher patiently gave him time to observe how the other students were rewarded both by her attention and by the attention of the class members themselves when they did their work without disturbing each other. Eventually, finding his own distracting behavior to be unrewarded and ignored, the new student began responding to signals in the way that the successful students were responding. His rewards were quick to follow!

The point I wish to make here is this: often as adults we do not have any one person to serve as our "model" in responding to certain tasks or responsibilities, for we are often in situations that are more or less unique to us. But what we can do is set forth an "ideal self" to serve as a kind of model which we in our rational moments help to construct. In effect we ask ourselves this basic question, "What would a sane, responsible, and reasonably happy person do on this job or in this situation?" Then we take the answers to this question and use them to serve as *signals to direct our own actual behavior.*

This model or "ideal self" is the sort of moral, rational, and happy being that we would like to be. Of course, even an "ideal self" should be constructed out of actual conditions. There is no practical point in setting up an ideal self that is excessively removed from what we actually are. We need a "model self" that we can think of as at least a genuine possibility for us to live up to. Later we can revise the ideal. Anna Young would have done well to ask herself the following question: "Given my present talents, opportunities, values, and training, what sort of responses should I make on this job if I want to be a sane, responsible, and reasonably happy person?"

The answer might have been, "First, I should go to the boss to ask that the job's signals and responsibilities be clarified. Then, I might show the boss the serious conflicts and confusions that are built into this job."

Of course, some bosses are not themselves very sane or responsible. But a wise employee, taking that fact into consideration, will ask, "What strategy would a sane, responsible, and happy person take to deal with this crazy job and the unresponsive boss?" It may be that a sane, responsible, and happy person can take some effective steps to make his or her own job more enjoyable and fruitful. Or, the rational conclusion might be either to look for another job, or to go over the boss' head, or simply to ignore certain signals on the job and leave them for the boss to respond to if the boss is unwilling to hire another person to help carry out the work.

In some cases, a person might conclude that in fact he or she has not been acting responsibly on the job even though the duties and signals are not in serious conflict. In short, if a person is suffering guilt, it may be because *of not living up to professed commitments.* If a person wants to be rid of this guilt, then that person must either shape up or reevaluate responses and duties.

To have guilt reactions is not necessarily undesirable. If we are doing wrong according to the standards that we are committed to, then guilt reactions may serve as alarm bells warning us that something has gone wrong and that we had better look into the matter. If we decide what a sane, responsible, and happy person would more likely do under a certain set of conditions, then we must *act that way ourselves* if we want to avoid judging ourselves to be either insane, irresponsible, or unhappy.

Breakdown in the Signal-Response-Reward System

As a finite creature you are not a spook existing independent of your physical and social environment. Your responses are an integral part of you. Take away your responses, and you will no longer be a vital human being. Depression often comes when there is a critical and sweeping breakdown in a person's signal-response-reward system. My college friends and I used to describe as "shot out of the saddle" any young man or woman who had just been told that his or her steady date no longer cared to maintain their close relationship. Because the couple had composed together a kind of signal-response-reward system that had been in effect for many months, the destruction of this system was sometimes quite shattering for especially the one who had been "shot out of the saddle." Usually, recovery came about, but not without some difficulty. Friends would gather around to help these unfortunate people by encouraging them to become attuned to *other* social signals. For example, instead of leaving the individuals alone to suffer their recent deprivation, they would invite these people to accompany them to basketball games. Or they might get them a date with new young persons. When one of my close friends broke up with the young woman whom he had known for a long time, I along with other friends found that we could help him cultivate new reinforcers and rewards. He in turn found that these new reinforcers helped him in coping with the fact that a major supply of his most meaningful supports had been removed from his life.

But if the person's friends failed to get him or her involved in another dynamic signal-response-reward system, then the individual was liable to sink into depression. Some people have killed themselves after the breakdown of an intense involvement with a member of the opposite sex. So being "shot out of the saddle" was and is no joking matter, as many parents have discovered when their children have come to report that they have lost their best girlfriend or boyfriend.

Because human life is not absolutely secure, an individual is less likely to be forced into a tailspin of depression if there is more than one signal-response-reward system to involve the person. Fortunately most people have many systems. For a person to expect either a job, spouse, church, hobby, or any other single finite reality to supply *all* the signals and rewards is unrealistic to the point of absurdity.

The Happiness Tax

Recently Marie Hamilton, on leave from hospitalization in a Neural-Psychiatric Clinic, reported to me that she had just had what might be the very best day of her entire life. She simply sat at a table and did some work on a painting that she had been *wanting* to do for a very long time. Nothing or no one seemed to threaten her. "Is this the way normal people have it?" she asked half jokingly but nevertheless seriously. I assured her that while many people have days without feeling personally threatened or unaccepted, most people have some bad days. Marie and I then talked about what I call the "Happiness Tax Theory."

According to this weird theory, if you are happy today, then you must pay a tax on it before the week comes to an end. You pay the tax by suffering. Most people pay off much of their Happiness Tax by having a time for feeling guilty. Marie seemed to think it necessary not only to pay this tax but, in her case, to be taxed four-fold. When she went through an entire day without being taxed, she did not know what it meant.

The Christian doctrine of grace says in effect that our most profound happiness is a divinely granted right in the sense that no one should have to suffer for simply being happy. Unfortunately, great numbers of people seem to believe that enjoyment is a sin no matter how the enjoyment comes about.

Two Kinds of Guilt

Guilt can be either appropriate or inappropriate. The latter is a wasteful, foolish, and pointless guilt. It does not make life more meaningful or moral. One recommended way to overcome this morbid and fruitless guilt is to challenge it directly by pronouncing judgment on it. Declare it insane. Label it as wasteful and stupid. Classify it as immoral.

This brings us to the first kind of guilt—appropriate guilt. It serves a very useful function in human life. There are times when we do real and actual harm to others and break the moral code. When we do this, we are in fact guilty and in need of forgiveness and repentance (i.e., change) so that the harmful deed or practice will not be repeated.

We do well to allow or even to train ourselves to feel guilty if we do harm to others. And I wish to add that we do well also to train ourselves to feel appropriate guilt when each of us does harm to *self* by indulging in *inappropriate and wasteful guilt*. In short, we must fight the foolish, stupid, and inappropriate guilt by declaring it to be an indecent waste of human happiness. The sooner we are rid of it, the better.

We may fight back in a second way. When we do act in such a way as to combine sanity, moral and social responsibility, and individual happiness for ourselves, then let us reward ourselves further by doing something that is both enjoyable to ourselves and harmless to others. For example, in the middle of the day on some Saturday, Peter may do something that he absolutely delights in doing—taking a bubble bath for an hour while reading a magazine or just closing his eyes and listening to music. Never mind that no one else in the neighborhood would enjoy doing this! If it is what Peter finds enjoyable, then that is sufficient.

Behavorism does not presume to tell each individual what is immediately rewarding to him, for people are very different. The point is that sane, responsible, and happy responses need to be reinforced or strengthened. They need to be rewarded. Some people would do well to write down a list of things that they would enjoy very much doing or experiencing. And if these things are not themselves judged to be either immoral or insane, then at least some of them should be made into positive reinforcers or rewards.

For example, when Karen goes through the entire Saturday without being sarcastic with her teen-age daughter, then Karen should reward herself well. Kindness has a hard enough time in the world. So why not strengthen it every time we can! If in good faith you think you have acted sanely or responsibly, or have overcome the threat of wasteful and inappropriate guilt, then reinforce these good qualities by rewarding yourself.

We have all heard people talk to themselves in the following way: "Oh, you dummy! Why did you do that?" I suggest that when we do something that is indeed foolish and crazy, we might do well to say to ourselves, "Well, *that's* a crazy thing to do." But note carefully: nothing was said about the *person as a whole*. Only one specific response or set of responses was designated as crazy. By the same token, when someone does something that is very successful or good, then why not let him say to himself, "That was a good job, Charles!" or "Superb work, Betty!" or even "Nice response, Jim." Praising one's own deeds and responses now and then can be quite practical and useful. Now and then I observe myself reading a line or two aloud, which helps to strengthen my silent reading. Similarly, complimenting or encouraging yourself aloud now and then may strengthen your good feelings about yourself. Indeed, according to the Apostle Paul, God is *for* us. So if the most Holy Being is for us, why should we be so arrogant as to be against ourselves!

Getting and Doing What You Want

In this chapter I have been concerned to deal with some methods that can be used for preventing or controlling depression. I have tried very much to avoid technical language or jargon. In this section of the chapter, I wish to set forth in everyday language a very significant point about depression.

When depression comes, it is often because people simply *cannot satisfy some of the wants and desires that they regard as very important to them*. When this happens to an excessive degree, the individual will tend to take new routes to get what he wants. This is quite normal and ordinary. But if the individual is frustrated at every turn, he or she may send out cries for help or even warnings to others to cease interfering with his or her plans; the depressed person may eventually give up by withdrawing.

Bart Cole was a graduate student who had been doing his work well. Unfortunately, his major professor seemed not to care whether Bart completed his degree and in fact threw unnecessary obstacles in Bart's path. In desperation, Bart tried to find out exactly what was required of him, but his professor gave him the runaround. Finally, determined that he was not going to be cheated out of his chance to earn his degree, Bart lay plans to sue his professor for malpractice. I venture to guess that most graduate students who suffer depression do so, not because of the work heaped upon them, but because there is little guidance and reason behind the work that they must do. I salute Bart for his persistence even though I am myself a professor who would not like being sued.

Anger, cries, pleas, rage—these forms of behavior are not yet manifestations of severe depression. But depression may follow unless some relief or satisfaction is found. Very simply, if a person's significant wants are constantly frustrated and if he cannot find new wants to replace the old ones, then he cannot continue in his miserable state. Something has to be done.

Withdrawal comes when a person says in effect that if he cannot get his significant wants satisfied—or at least *some* of them satisfied—then *he might as well not have any wants.* Depression *is* the state in which the major wants and desires themselves begin to burn down and extinguish one by one. It is death on the installment plan.

Reinforcing the Grounds for Hope

But we usually resist death with everything we have. In fact, if individuals cannot gain satisfaction of those wants that are most significant to them, they may begin to act as if suffering or frustration is what they "really want." People gain at least *some* satisfaction in having the option to suffer or to be frustrated. If nothing else, suffering is an indication that one is still alive.

Psychotherapists and psychiatrists often deal with clients who fiercely resist any attempt to change their pattern of frustration or suffering. The reason is that these clients have lost the hope of ever being able to live without a flood of frustration and hurts. They have learned to be strangely comfortable with their steady state of misery and do not want to run the risk of upsetting at least the predictable life of suffering. If anything is worse than predictable suffering, it is *un*predictable suffering of a devastating kind. A person may be able to handle an expected amount of suffering. By expecting not to get well, he can at least escape the form of destructive suffering that comes in having one's *hopes* destroyed. He lives on the assumption that having little or no hope of recovery or improvement is far better than getting his hopes lifted high only to have them dashed to pieces.

Ministers, therapists, and counselors have found that talking someone out of a level of depression is not easy. Sometimes it is impossible to do so. Many people in depression may strongly *resist talking* about it because it is so difficult to "communicate the feeling of mental pain in terms adequate to be understood."[5] Indeed, failure in the attempt to communicate it may drive the individual still deeper into depression. Sometimes when the person does risk talking about it, he or she is met with condescending remarks from people who simply do not understand how the depressed feel or what they are going through. So, why add insult to injury? If "opening up" provides an occasion to be hurt again, then it is safer to remain shut tight.

It is very easy to lose patience with the depressed individual. In order to understand the situation better, we might compare it to very poor people who live on the economic margin. What they earn each month gives them bare subsistence but nothing for saving or investing. A person who has plenty of money may regard investing to be a "normal" part of living. He or she may not be able to understand someone who simply refuses to invest money now and then. But the poor people living on the margin see that it would be foolish to risk investing. In the first place, they cannot afford it. In the second place, if they should lose their investment, it would be a disaster. Similarly, the severely depressed individuals living on the margin, look upon the investment of new hopes and dreams to be an absurd risk. If they lose again, they may be wiped out completely. They reason that it is better to live in dire emotional and functional poverty than to take a chance on being eliminated once and for all by still another disappointment. Those who have a surplus in life can afford to risk themselves emotionally and in other ways, for they have extra "capital" to fall back on in case they lose their investment.

It may, therefore, be a cruel thing to inspire a depressed friend or relative to take a chance on hoping once again. It is more practical and humane to build some reasonably firm and secure supports before asking the person to venture out again. Still, when we have built these supports, we will not likely see the depressed person move. We can avoid impatience at this point by looking at the situation from the depressed person's viewpoint. What seems to be reasonable security from our perspective, may appear to be too risky from his or her perspective.

Therefore, we may have to add still more supports until, in *his or her* mind, the new venture will not likely wipe him or her out emotionally and functionally. In other words, it takes more than words to encourage a severely depressed individual. It take solid ground to venture out on.

Behaviorism and the Constant Complainer

Unlike some techniques of therapy, behaviorism does not emphasize "talking through" one's problems. Sometimes insight is useful and sometimes not. According to behaviorists, if we listen to a moderately depressed person complain and groan continually, we are actually rewarding, reinforcing, or strengthening the perpetuation of this pattern. Listening for long stretches of time may be advisable to begin with, but beyond a point it strengthens perpetual complaining as a life-style. Therefore, behaviorists try to observe very carefully any *other* constructive behavior—no matter how slight—that the depressed individual manifests. Immediately the behaviorist will reinforce this other response by whatever appropriate reward. At the same time, the behaviorist will gradually reduce the amount of attention and reward that he gives to the complainer's talk about his misery. In fact, the behaviorist may eventually ignore almost all his client's

complaining in order to *attend to the more constructive responses*—
even the slightest ones.

By use of behavioristic techniques, a person in depression
may be able to *condition himself or herself* in such a way as to
overcome depression. What is important about behaviorism is its
insistence that the human individual is a dependent creature. This
is certainly in keeping with the Christian teaching of human finitude. The claim that an individual can solve problems only by
drawing on inner strength is a claim more of Stoicism than of
either Christianity or behaviorism.

Suppose You Are the One Getting Depressed

If you are severely depressed all the time, you would not be
reading this chapter. But you may have periods of depression,
sometimes severe and sometimes not so severe. Even if a person
is depressed only once a month, it is something that he wants
very much to overcome. I have not experienced a day of depression in twenty-five years. But the memories of the savage depression that I suffered as a teen-ager and youth are sufficient to help
me appreciate the horror that my friends suffer when they fall into their slough of hopeless dejection. I would not for two million
dollars repeat the fifteenth year of my life. Those who have never
known real depression cannot begin to imagine what the terrible
experience is like.

Behavorism admits that often it is impossible to know what
causes a particular person's depression. Peeling back the layers of
one's past in order to get at the "source" of the problem could
take years of analysis. Behavioral therapists, therefore, say that
you do not always need to know how you got into a mess in
order to get out of it.

Take the case of Martha Hamilton, who sank into deep
depression each afternoon at about 5:00 and did not emerge until
7:00 P.M. If you are in depression a lot, observe yourself enough
to find out *when* it happens and *where* it happens. Martha observed that she fell into this state no matter where she was. So,
going out to eat rather than staying home to cook after her depression was over did not help at all.

What caused Martha to become depressed at this particular time? No one knows. But let us suppose for the moment that we do know. As a child her father used to come home at 5:00 P.M. In that particular family, it was the father's job to administer punishment to the children. The mother, therefore, simply told little Martha that her father would discipline her when he came home. Upon arriving at 5:00 P.M., the father was told about the misbehavior of the children. Family arguments and scoldings ensued and the punishment was administered.

This imaginary scene is typical of a number of families. Many children actually come to *expect* punishment on a more or less regular schedule. When the children reach a certain age, their parents may have to give up punishing them, but the pattern of *expecting to be punished* is not so easily given up by the offspring. Psychoanalysis and family studies show that punishment-structures can be identified in families and that these structures shape considerably the life-patterns of individuals even after they leave home.

Realizing that in most cases it is practically impossible to determine what all the major causes of any individual's periods of depression are, the behavioral therapist seeks to find a plan of action rather than an explanation. Let us assume that you are in Martha's situation, what plan of action would you set forth in order to deal with the depression if you were a behaviorist? You would, first of all, ask what you would *prefer* to do or experience between 5:00 and 7:00 P.M. in the place of suffering depression. Behavioral therapists use the phrase "target behavior" to refer to the desirable responses and experiences to shoot for in self-modification. "The basic idea in self-modification is to arrange situations so that desirable behavior is positively reinforced [or rewarded] and unwanted behavior is not reinforced."[6]

For example, instead of desiring the depression from 5:00 to 7:00 P.M., you would desire to be preparing the evening meal and enjoying it with the family. Of course, not every desire is sane, responsible, or conducive to happiness. But a quick check suggests that preparing and enjoying a family meal meets the test of what a sane, responsible, and happy person might do in your situation if you were Martha. (In a later chapter I will discuss vocational options for women. There is no biblical basis for thinking that God ordained women rather than men to work in kitchens.) There are many other constructive alternatives for Martha, but this alternative of cooking and enjoying the meal is sufficient to show how behavioral therapy could be applied to one's own case.

Note that in setting up the target behavior of the meal, you are not wasting time on directly eliminating depression responses but rather are spending time on strengthening other responses that are worthwhile in their own right. The behavioral tactic here is to strengthen the behavior that is itself desirable and responsible so that it may eliminate the undesirable behavior from the picture. In other words, the plan is to *starve the depression behavior* by simply ignoring it and giving all the rewards to the desirable and constructive behavior that you want to develop at the very time that the depression behavior has been occurring.

Shaping Your Own Behavior

One tactic used by behaviorism is called "shaping." If you cannot yet engage in any constructive activity between 5:00 to 7:00 P.M. because of the depression, then perhaps you can begin enacting your plan at some other time of the day or night. For example, during the early afternoon (when you are not depressed), you might take off 10 or 15 minutes to write down a list of things that you find pleasant or enjoyable to do. Then reward yourself for writing down the list. The following is just the beginning of a possible list of desirable things you might draw up:

> going to a play, picnic, movie, or concert
> going downtown
> taking a ride in the country
> reading a novel
> climbing a mountain
> visiting with Jane and Ted
> eating Mexican food
> browsing in the library

spending an hour on Saturday alone with your spouse in
   order to listen to soft music
painting a picture
visiting the flower show
playing with the dog
watching football on television
being served breakfast in bed
buying that FM radio you have been wanting
singing in the choir
playing the guitar
loafing for an entire hour, etc.

Your particular list of desirable things turns out to be a
list of things that will serve as rewards or reinforcers for you.
They can be used to *strengthen any response which you make that
moves you in the direction of going to the kitchen to cook and eat
between 5:00 and 7:00 P.M.* For example, suppose that during
your period of depression you get up and *walk half-way* to the
kitchen rather than remain back in your bedroom. If you do this
on Monday, then try to reward yourself then and there. If you
cannot, then try writing down on a piece of paper a promise that
later in the evening you will give yourself one of the rewards that
you have written down. It is best to reward yourself *immediately
after* responding in the constructive way. But if you cannot, then
do so as soon as possible.

If you are Martha, you usually prepare the evening meal
after 7:00 P.M.—after your cloud of depression has been lifted.
So, on Monday at about 9:00 P.M. (when you are okay), ask
your spouse to bring you a reward. Knowing how well you like
Mexican food, you ask him or her—or one of your children—to
bring from the Mexican restaurant a delicious, super-special meal
and have it ready for you *sharply at 6:45 P.M.* Then if you walk
to the kitchen at this terrible time—which is 15 minutes before
your depression is usually *over*—then you will get to eat the excellent Mexican meal even if you have to take it back into the bedroom to eat.

What you are doing here is *strengthening any behavior that will get you up and out of the room in which you retire for your period of depression.* You are acting as your own coach and are focusing on the movements or responses that help you to get to your eventual target behavior. The rule is: *no movement is too small to start with.* If you cannot make one move, then perhaps you can make another and smaller one. If so, make it and then reward yourself. Try to arrange in advance to have the rewards already waiting on you.

One of the advantages of behaviorism is that it focuses on behavior and not on a lot of so-called "inner complexes." It emphasizes that the trouble is with the responses (or behavior) in connection with the signals and the consequences. The responses or signals or consequences should be dealt with directly. For a behaviorist, even your *talking* about a plan of action is already an *example* of a constructive response. So reward it. It is an improvement when you talk about a plan of *action* rather than complain. This improvement needs to be strengthened. Then, when even a small step of the plan is enacted, reward it; for it, too, needs strengthening. And so you move from reward to reward.

It is imperative to understand that, for behaviorists, any response you make counts as behavior. This means that any response that moves you toward the target is progress and is perhaps needful of reinforcement. Instead of asking "*Why* am I depressed?" a behaviorist will usually ask, "*What* is my next step to move me toward my target behavior? *What* can I use to reward or strengthen my taking this step, or at least this half a step?"

Usually, the time to map out a plan and to set up rewards and their means of distribution is when you are in a free state of mind. You may need to ask a family member or a friend to give you the proper *signal* to take the first step. You may even need him to give you the subsequent *reward*. Or you may find some other way. For example, you may at 4:00 P.M. set your alarm clock in the bedroom to ring at 6:00 P.M. That will be your signal to, say, rinse your face in cool water, turn on the light, or do something else concrete that will move you toward the kitchen before 7:00 P.M. and eventually move you to walk in by 5:00 P.M. in order to begin preparing the meal.

Review

There are many more things that could be said about how behaviorism works to move a depressed person toward behavior that is sane, responsible, and enjoyable. But I trust that enough has been said in this chapter to give a fair notion of what can be done about the withdrawal responses which we call depression. Perhaps the best contribution of behaviorism is its attitude of "Divide and Conquer!" In effect, behaviorists say that we human mortals are a lot of responses (at least), some of which are just too big to control. But by dividing them into smaller responses, we stand a much better chance of getting a foot in the door, so to speak. Depression is, after all, a lot of responses. But if we can eliminate or transform *some* of the depression responses, then by an effective use of rewards, we might be able to weaken the collective impact of a certain complex of responses which we call depression.

How Do You See Yourself?

In the Introduction to this book, I promised to draw from two major schools of therapy in dealing with the problem of depression. They were the school of behavioral therapy and the school of cognitive therapy. However, Karl R. Popper, one of the most respected living philosophers, has pointed out that the subject matter of human behavior is not the private domain of any school or any field or any department in a university. Basically, there are just problems to be dealt with, and from anyone or any school of research we may learn whatever we can that has vital bearing on a given problem.[7]

There is little doubt that behavioral therapy has made some remarkable progress in helping people to overcome severe depression. What I wish to do in this last section is to explore the claim of the cognitive therapists that depression often develops and becomes ingrained because of *costly misconceptions about ourselves*. Or, to translate this insight of the cognitists into the language of behavioral therapy, people sometimes misunderstand the interrelationships between their own responses and their environment. Socrates was told "Know thyself!" But it is impractical to suppose that an individual can just know self. There is just too much to know. What we can become acquainted with is *some of our responses and experiences in relationship to significant cues and reinforcers,* including those given by other people.

Dr. Albert Ellis is a psychotherapist who claims that often some people are depressed because they think that certain responses are *inevitable or required* when in reality they are neither. It took Martin Keats ten years of his adult life to realize finally that he did not have to be a minister just because his parents had raised him to become a minister. The parents may have had this requirement, but it was not inevitable that Martin Keats himself make it a requirement.

Some behaviorists insist that insight comes by carefully observing the most influential reinforcing experiences that go into shaping an individual's life. We have little difficulty in understanding that certain individuals break out with a rash or allergy when they are in the presence of certain kinds of plants. Similarly, we can observe how people develop very severe fear-reactions or anxiety-reactions, and even depression, when they are in the presence of certain *social stimuli.* Insight sometimes comes when the undesirable reaction is observed and the signals and reinforcers of the reaction are also identified and tested.

Through a process of association, as well as other processes which need not be explored here, people build up double and triple reactions to certain kinds of social stimuli. This process has beneficial as well as harmful consequences. I will clarify this a bit. If someone from the eighteenth century were suddenly to drop into your home town, he or she would "see" the red traffic light, but it would not have the same "meaning" that it has for you and me. That is, this person would not respond or react in the way that you and I do regularly. Over the years, you and I have, fortunately, been "conditioned" to stop at red lights. This conditioning process is to our benefit and to the benefit of others who drive and walk in our neighborhood.

But suppose that you have been well trained in the restaurant business. Each time a customer comes in, you immediately begin looking alert, picking up a menu, and finding the customer a place to sit. If trained by a very conscientious manager, you would watch carefully but discreetly to see how the customers are doing. Do they need more coffee or tea? Do they need fresh water? And so on. Now, suppose that you are yourself invited out to *eat* at a plush restaurant. Normally, a person would enjoy this experience. But because of your training, you might find yourself being hyper-alert, making little initial responses literally with your body when new customers come into the restaurant in which you are seated as a customer yourself. You cannot help wondering who will seat the new customers. And so on. On the whole, because the cues and signals in a restaurant have for so many years served literally to *move your body into action,* you find that going out to eat is simply not relaxing to you. Your body seems coiled to spring into action. You cannot sit there oblivious to the cues and signals all about you.

Now, there is nothing "crazy" about you. There is nothing "wrong" with you in some deep and profound sense. You simply are a victim of a special kind of training that made you alert and sensitive to certain signals. In order to overcome this disadvantage, you might need to go through some sort of desensitizing so that your responses, when you go out to eat, will be more enjoyable to you. You will have to learn not to *expect* to be sensitive to the restaurant cues.

Because of the way they grew up, many people have responses which, in their present situations, are very harmful to them. They have *expectations of themselves that are unrealistic,* or they *expect from their environment consequences that they have no sound reason to expect.* I was told that many TV stars who receive all sorts of recognition in the United States become quite upset and "blue" during their stay in Europe, where few recognize them or ask for their autographs. Instead of wondering what is wrong with themselves, however—or what is wrong with the Europeans—the TV stars need simply to see that it is only reasonable to expect that Europeans will not recognize them. To *expect otherwise* is simply unrealistic and fruitless. The cognitive therapists state that a large number of their clients are suffering severe anxiety and even depression because they try to run their lives on the basis of drastically unrealistic expectations about either their own behavior or the behavior of others.

The common-sense therapist Albert Ellis says that much unnecessary failure and depression comes to people who have not yet learned (1) what to expect from the physical environment, (2) what to expect their own personal responses to be, and (3) what responses to expect from other people. For example, a number of people feel *rejected* because they, quite unrealistically, expect that everyone whom they meet ought to like them or find them to be interesting. They erroneously conclude that because *some* people dislike them or do not find them interesting, then they must surely be disliked by *everyone* and are uninteresting to everyone. However, instead of stating their problem in this way, the depressed person will often say, "I'm not a very likeable *person. I'm not an intersting being."* Dr. Ellis would teach the depressed to be more accurate in such self-descriptions. Behaviorists recommend that we talk, not of ourselves as a person or being, but of ourselves as *responses* and *experiences.* This is not because we are not persons, but because being a person is such a complex thing. We cannot observe *all* of us! But we can focus on some of the responses and experiences more relevant and pertinent to the problem we are dealing with.

Let us, however, suppose that Carl Hooper really is uninteresting to *everyone* he meets. Still, it does not realistically follow that he *must* be uninteresting. In other words, the past is not the whole of reality. His present-future responses do not have to be a ditto copy of his past responses, for the present and future have resources that may not have been available in the past. Some people who fail in so many of their undertakings explain, "Well, that's the way I *am!*" Existentialists and others would shoot back by saying, "No, that's the way you *have been* in the past. Now, however, what are you going to do about the present and future?"

Dr. Ellis claims that people often predict for themselves disasters that they have no basis for predicting. In doing this, they do bring to the real situation a *new factor*. That is, they bring in the prediction itself, the prediction of disaster. This prediction often becomes itself a *causal* factor in helping to bring about the disaster. If these people could substitute some factor other than a prediction of disaster, they might in some cases supply what is needed to change the real situation so that the disaster will not happen.

Some people, however, like to be able to say, "Well, I failed again, but I knew I would. I predicted it." If this is what a person *wants,* then that individual is successful in at least one thing—predicting his or her own failures. This may be a source of great comfort, However, if an individual wants something other than this, then the person will have to become sufficiently realistic to see that in some situations any man or woman *might* and *must* fail. The difference is that in a case of must fail, there are no plans or steps one can take to bring about better consequences. The fate is sealed. On the other hand, if one only *might* fail, then there is the chance of bringing in some intervening variables to help tip the scales in favor of success.

For example, Betty Newton has just moved into a new neighborhood in Houston and does not know anyone. Instead of wondering how long it will be before she makes friends in her new town, she decides that she, after all, does have some options. She knows that she will be going to church Sunday, but she does not know how friendly the church members are. What can she *do*?

Some sociological and psychological studies indicate that depression for a number of people seems to come with a move from one town to another. This does not mean that depression is inevitable. It does mean, however, that depressed individuals may not have taken advantage of some of the options and choices available to them in helping them to adjust to the new situation.

In Betty's situation, she has the option of calling the church during the week to find out what it has for new people. Or, she can go to the church office on a weekday to meet some of the staff members. She can even find out who her son's or daughter's Sunday School teacher will be and what the teacher's phone number is. Perhaps the teacher will be a friendly person. It turns out that Betty has all sorts of options. To predict failure in making new friends is certainly not warranted by any significant body of facts in her situation. The facts seem to allow Betty a considerable amount of room for making a number of plans and putting them into action.

Dr. Ellis makes another very practical point. People sometimes become depressed, not because their heart's major desire fails to gain satisfaction, but because they expect that if this desire does fall through, then *everything* will be lost. Teenage theatrics are sometimes expressed in this mode of thought. If a boy loses out in his romance, he thinks his entire world had collapsed. It helps to see that while the hurt is genuine and the loss is quite serious, nevertheless there are things that can be done to help cope with the defeat and loss.

In common sense terms, depression is often the result of bad logic or poor reasoning. We expect responses from ourselves which we have no realistic basis for expecting. Or, by contrast, we sometimes predict absolute failure for ourselves even when there is no basis for thinking that our fateful prediction is more realistic than a more favorable prediction. Also depression comes by not being able to focus on other alternatives when our first or second alternative fails to deliver. Ellis would have us *practice* looking at problems (easy ones to begin with) and then imaginatively coming up with a *number* of possible alternatives for dealing with them.

This section on "How Do You See Yourself?" may be summarized under two basic points. First, in some cases depression can be better handled by developing (through practice) the *skill* of more accurately observing your own responses and the consequences of the environment (both social and physical) on those responses. Second, there is another skill that can be improved by practice. It is the skill of imagining more alternatives for dealing with difficult problems, including depression. Realistic thinking requires not only careful and hard-nosed observation of what *is*, but bold and daring imagination of what *might come to be* if certain actions are taken. We are what we are now, but we do not know now all the responses that we will be making in the future. This is because we do not know what signals and reinforcers will reside in our environment tomorrow and in the more remote future. Fortunately, it is possible to begin now to change or modify some future signals and reinforcers of tomorrow.

Sometimes an individual who is depressed goes to a minister or therapist for help. In doing so, he is in effect acting constructively to change some of tomorrow's environment. The minister, therapist, or understanding friend becomes, among other things, a set of important signals and reinforcers which could just help turn depressive situations into ones that are more constructive and meaningful.

In other chapters of this book I will be drawing heavily from either cognitive therapy or behavioral psychology, as the situation or topic of discussion demands. Let us turn now to explore some of what Christians, with their special values and commitments, may expect in today's world.

II

WHEN
CHRISTIANS ENCOUNTER
THEIR OWN SEXUALITY

Sexual Happiness in Marriage

In his very practical book *Sexual Happiness in Marriage*, Herbert J. Miles has sought to help a number of Christians "to achieve a healthy and satisfying sexual relationship."[1] In effect, by calling on both special and general revelation, he has sought to teach them to approach the sexual adventure with a sense of anticipation and skill rather than fear and anxiety. In the Old Testament the marvelous book entitled Song of Songs is filled with delightful love-talk between human beings, but many of the Church fathers missed the point by trying to make of it a disguised "spiritual" dialogue between Christ and his Church, or between God and Israel. By purging legitimate sexual enjoyment from the Bible, these Church fathers revealed more about their own hang-ups than about God's wishes for married couples. But Christians who desire to make their sexual intimacy more satisfying might together read the Song of Songs. Some religions may wish to take the sexual experience out of the religious life, but this should not be true of Christianity. The Bible is not so flat and prosaic a book as some people have imagined.

In times past, many sincere believers regarded as sinful the use of contraceptives. While prohibitions against adultery and fornication appear in both the Old and New Testaments, this fact should not have led Christians to suppose that God was against sexual enjoyment and pleasure within the bond of marriage. Many Christians used to believe — and a few still do — that sexual intercourse between husband and wife is solely for procreation. Or at least it was assumed that unless a married couple had in mind to make the wife pregnant, they had no right to *enjoy* the sexual relationship. But as Christians and others moved from the farm to the city, they began to give birth to fewer children. It is doubtful that they began to have less sexual intimacy, which suggests that a number of Christians began suffering guilt because they were engaging in the sexual act without intending to have children. It is pretty difficult to have sexual intercourse without enjoying it, although some people seem to manage to take the joy out of it, or at least they pretend to do so in order not to seem wicked to their spouses or to themselves.

Nowhere does the Bible clearly teach that sexual intercourse between husband and wife should be enjoyed only if they have in mind to replenish the earth. God told Adam and Eve to *multiply*. But that was surely a limited commandment; for, after all, there was no population explosion in those days. Christians have sometimes done themselves and others a disservice by taking a local or temporary biblical commandment to be either universal in scope or wholly insensitive to what can be learned through other legitimate means.

With This Wondrous Body

The writer of Genesis stated that God made man — male and female — and declared his creation to be good. We like to believe that each part of the human body is also appropriately good. When the daughter of Jack and Lisa McClelland was about three years of age, the parents received a phone call from a friendly neighbor telling them that their daughter Sandy was completely naked in the front yard. It was the month of May, and she had climbed a tree and was enjoying the experience of waving at the cars passing by the house. When Jack called to her and motioned for her to come to him, little Sandy eased down the tree and ran about ten or fifteen strides toward her father, stopped, spread her legs and arms wide and announced with child-like delight, "Look, Daddy, I'm *barefooted!*"

Both Jack and Lisa had taken care not to communicate negative signals to their daughter that her body was evil. She was totally unaware of being completely in the nude and was thrilled only by the realization that for the first time during the year she had gone outside the house barefooted.

Naturally, Jack could not permit Sandy to remain naked in the front yard, but at the same time he had no interest in making her feel ashamed of her body. So her father said simply, "If you put on some clothes, you won't skin your nice body on the rough tree." Upon getting into her clothes, she returned to her tree.

Jack and Lisa never had to teach Sandy to wear clothes; she simply observed others and gradually picked up the practice. Her parents simply complimented her pretty clothing — as well as her pretty body. But they made no idol of either clothes or body.

Their son, Jonathan, on the other hand, was probably taught by someone at school that he should never be seen naked, not even at the age of six. In fact, he became very prudish until he and his father had a light discussion about the human body. Jack named a few things that Jonathan's body was good for — jumping, kicking, and throwing. Jonathan then added swimming and whistling. Jack concluded for him that their bodies must be a very wonderful thing to have. "I don't know what I'd do without mine," Jack said to his son. And they together continued to talk lightly but seriously of the advantages of having a good body. Today, Jonathan is "modest" about his body, but he was able to avoid becoming excessively prudish and ashamed of his body.

The Embrace

Unfortunately, some people grow up with confused and mixed feelings about their own bodies. When they marry, this confusion is sometimes intensified. When infants come into the world, most of those mothers who hold their infants do so by placing them on the mother's left side. Many students of the parent-child relationship hold that this practice keeps the tiny babe in touch with the mother's heartbeat and provides the child the body reinforcement that is essential to both security and stimulation. As the infant grows into childhood, the embrace between parent and child is still one of the most moving experiences of human existence. Then when children hit the teenage period, they are often cut off from parental embraces and are advised not to embrace each other as young people. I recall that as a boy of thirteen one of my aunts and I would engage in very playful wrestling. This was, among other things, a form of healthy body contact. Like many other children growing up, I did lots of wrestling with other kids, which provided body contact, too. Fortunately, there were uncles and older cousins who regularly would pat me on the head or shoulder. But what of those children and youths who are cut off from all healthy and gentle physical contacts?

It is easy to see how some people might come to think that physical contact even between husband and wife is a "weakness of the flesh." By contrast, as a boy, I used to wonder why it was that so many married people whom I knew did not seem to like each other physically. Of course, I was unable to verbalize this youthful puzzlement. Fortunately, one couple — a delightful uncle and aunt whom I sometimes stayed with in the summer — were frequently playful with each other. Sometimes they reminded me of pups playing together in the back yard. Despite the fact that in their religion they were very strict Fundamentalists, they did not find anywhere in the Bible a prohibition against husband and wife taking pleasure in each other's physical bodies. I count it as a very fortunate "break" in life for me that I was able to see and hear my Christian aunt and uncle delight in playfully kissing and embracing one another.

Degrees of Passion

Not all sexuality has to be deadly serious and intensely passionate. I am sure that when alone, my uncle and aunt could be powerfully passionate. But they did not think that loving sexually had to be enjoyed at just one level of intensity or even in one position. For some reason, some Christians have developed the strange notion that there is just one sexual organ for the male and one sexual organ for the woman. This is carrying specialization to a ridiculous extreme! I could actually *see* my aunt and uncle express their loving sexuality through their hands and arms as well as their playing eyebrows and contagious laughs. I could *hear* their sexual talk. They did keep their sexual communication light in public, or when I was in the house with them. But even at this light level, their versatility was still pleasant to behold and hear.

The Human Body in Relationship

Compared to the confused and ambivalent Victorian attitude toward the human body, the Bible's more wholesome attitude will appear to us as a fresh and pleasant breeze. The writer of Psalm 51:8 freely speaks of his *bones* rejoicing. In the Old Testament the most frequently used word referring to the entire person is *basar*, which is best translated as *flesh*. As Dwight Hervey Small points out, it was some of the church fathers, not the biblical writers themselves, who came to view the human body of flesh, blood, and bone as something of a vile appendage to the soul, an appendage which was thought to be a curse and a cause of shame.[2]

The biblical view of male and female is that human individuals have their being *in relationship* with other persons. Because persons are unique and are different from one another, the relationships that hold between persons will not all be the same. For example, the relationship between an individual and his God will be considerably different from that between himself and his wife, or between himself and his mother. Nevertheless, the Christian view is that to be a person is to be in *relationship* with other persons.

In all human relationships the body is absolutely essential for even minimal communications and expression. The relationship between parent and child enjoys a wholesome physical contact that is both meaningful in itself and essential to the physical and emotional growth of the child. Between husband and wife, physical contact can be a profound human relationship. Sexual responses of varying degrees and levels are one of the deepest rewards of marital life.

But honest Christians must face the hard and practical question of sexual arousal that comes, despite everything, to an individual who is not married. Should this individual rush out to get married in order to gain relief from this unintended sexual arousal? It is quite likely that such a drastic solution would cause more moral problems than it could solve, and so, we are back where we started. What about those Christian men and women who suffer an upsurge of sexual passion even though they are not married? It is only right that they be offered a decent and understanding option.

The Question of Masturbation

In the days of the patriarchs or even of the Christian apostles, young people were prone to marry quite early, many years before our young people today marry. Hence, the stressful period of "waiting" before having a sexually intimate relationship was not for them so serious a problem as it is for contemporary Christians. It is only modern social and cultural conditions that lead us to expect our youths to postpone marrying and having sexual relationships until after they become eighteen or older. Biologically, young people are ready for the sexual experience in at least their early teens.

In dealing with the question of masturbation for Christians, I would like to stress that the Bible does not teach that masturbation is sinful. When we consult sources outside the Bible we are forced again to conclude that there is no basis for the charge that masturbation is itself evil or harmful. To be sure, there are many old wives' tales and other fictions about the harm that masturbation can do, but the evidence of medical and psychological studies shows that the taboo against it is very misguided. Indeed in his book *Whatever Became of Sin?* Dr. Karl Menninger shows that false and misleading statements about the woes and evils of masturbation have done untold psychological harm to young people.[3] As the Christian sociologist Dr. Herbert Miles states, "There is no scientific evidence that masturbation is biologically harmful."[4]

There is absolutely no excuse for concerned Christians' delaying aid to those many sincere Christians who have been made to suffer destructive feelings of guilt about the act of masturbation. Many believers are tormented needlessly and unmercifully because their earnest prayers for deliverance from masturbation seem not to have been answered with "the victory." Sometimes these people think that God has placed on them a special curse for their lack of self-restraint and self-control. But what can be done to put a stop to these misguided and wasteful ways of thinking and its accompanying agony?

The first thing that can be done is to put the whole question of masturbation in *biblical perspective* instead of allowing Christian lives to be harassed by a pseudo-morality that gets in the way of genuine morality. The Bible sets masturbation in proper perspective by *not even discussing or mentioning the topic at all.* That is how unimportant the entire matter was to the biblical writers!

Unfortunately, many centuries ago some commentators took the story of Onan in Genesis 38:8-10 to be a reference to masturbation. They even went so far as to claim that God struck Onan dead for committing one act of masturbation. However, a careful and unbiased reading of the biblical story itself reveals that the subject does not even enter the picture. To make this story an attack against masturbation per se is to miss the entire point of the story.

Christian morality requires that a clear distinction be made between (1) *real or objective* guilt and (2) the mere *feeling* of guilt. A person can be objectively guilty of an immoral act even though the individual may not *feel* guilty. At the same time, a person may *feel* guilty despite the fact that an actual immoral act has not been committed. Christians who feel guilty about masturbation must be helped to see that their feeling is not itself a basis of real or objective guilt. In short, they need to change their feeling to fit the objective reality. The energy spent in feeling guilty about so unimportant a matter as masturbation should be spent on something that contributes more to the Christian calling. To agonize over the act of masturbation is to dwell on the unimportant. Christians who worry about masturbation could place it in perspective by noting that in practically every society, certain harmless acts have been mistakenly branded as earth-shaking.

Christians are to be cautioned against swallowing the taboos and prohibitions of the society that they happened to have been born in. Among the Navajo Indians, it is considered to be an evil thing for a person to meet his or her mother-in-law face to face. If a Navajo should somehow talk face to face with the mother-in-law but not recognize who she is, nothing would happen unless that person should later learn that he or she had indeed talked face to face with her. But if at a later time the person should learn this, the individual would then suffer untold guilt and fear.

We find it very difficult to understand the agony that the Navajo would suffer over breaking this ancient taboo, but the masturbation taboo seems to be in the same class with the mother-in-law taboo. The earthly globe is riddled with taboos that torment individuals, usually for no good reason.

Therefore, instead of wasting prayer and meditation time brooding over this relatively insignificant human phenomenon of masturbation, the Christian would do well to turn to more rewarding prayers and meditations.

Christ said that to look lustfully upon a woman is comparable to committing adultery. We would be going too far to claim that Jesus had in mind to include masturbation in this condemnation. Some Christian theologians are now debating seriously the question of whether looking on a woman to lust after her includes having *mental images* of the opposite sex. We could easily agree that such mental images might be condemned if they invariably *lead* to the attempt to commit the overt act of adultery. But some Christian moral philosophers have advanced a very strong argument for the view that masturbation may

actually provide the needed relief that *prevents adultery or fornication.*[5]

I have argued that the most practical way of coping with
irrational guilt feelings about masturbation is for the Christian
to set the act of masturbation in proper biblical perspective and
to remind oneself now and then that *feeling* guilty is not to be
confused with *being* guilty. The next practical step that the
Christian can take is that of cultivating a healthy sense of humor.
In all the earth, no other creature possesses the marvelous human
capacity to laugh. The committed Christian, therefore, should
use this creative gift against pseudo-moralities and against other
forces which frustrate creative Christain living. Martin Luther
used to laugh aloud at the devil, and today Christians can laugh
at themselves when they take so insignificant an act as masturbation and turn it into a cosmic ordeal! They can laugh aloud at
their own foolishness, just as Elijah laughed at the prophets of
Baal.

Finally, if dedicated Christians find that much of their
prayer and meditation time is dominated by worrying about
masturbation, they may wish to write down a long list of important topics to pray and meditate about. The topic of masturbation can be left off and ignored. By using this tactic, the
Christian may eventually eliminate feelings of shame regarding
masturbation; for, after all, there are far more important and
interesting things to pray, meditate, and think about.

If I were the devil, I would try to upset Christian young
people by making them feel guilty about all sorts of harmless
activities. In this way, these young Christians would devote so
much attention to the unimportant things, they would not give
attention to their Christian duties and joys. It is time to be
truthful: many devout Christians do now, and will continue
to, masturbate without doing harm to either themselves or anyone.
It is only right, therefore, that the real blame be turned upon
those to whom it belongs—namely, those writers who, with
neither biblical authority nor medical and psychological evidence,
arrogantly take upon themselves to declare masturbation a sin.
The Christian is under no divine command to give heed to such

self-appointed censors. Therefore, when unmarried Christian young men or women select masturbation as an alternative to sexual intercourse outside the commitments of marriage, each has a perfect right to rejoice that he or she has found a way to carry on the Christian pilgrimage without violating the seventh commandment. The taboo against masturbation grows out of the pagan tradition which declared all sexuality to be vile and evil. Christians may be thankful that their own tradition is more discriminating and positive than the pagan tradition.

III

WHEN CHRISTIANS FACE THE QUESTION OF ABORTION

The Case of Betty Norton

Betty Norton, forty-two years old, did not go to college. But now that her youngest son is doing well in high school, she dearly wants to attend college. Having served her family well for many years, she now wants to do something in addition to raising children. Realizing that there is a wide world of interests awaiting her eager mind, she enthusiastically enrolls in the university. To be sure, she is a bit anxious. After all, it has been twenty-four years since she was in school as a student, and she has heard two of her children as well as her friends talk about taking tests and writing term papers at the university. Despite her fears and uncertainties, however, Betty knows that the university experience is going to be a new avenue of freedom and enrichment for her. Her husband, Mark, has even arranged to take one seminar with her on Thursday evenings. Her high-school son, James, playfully teases her about his having his mom as a coed when he gets to college two years from now.

After a month of her new venture at the university, Betty settles down in her studies and proves to herself that she does indeed have intellectual discipline and promise. Wisely, she had decided earlier to take only three courses instead of the "normal" four courses; for, after all, she still has responsibilities at home, even though they are much lighter than they were when the house was filled with the utterances and demands of small children.

One day, however, after suffering some nagging suspicions, Betty learns from her physician that she is pregnant. The news comes as a powerful blow to her. She scolds herself for not having had herself sterilized; but being somewhat conservative in temperament, she has simply been unable to take what was to her a most radical and drastic step. Mark is now also feeling guilty over his wife's new pregnancy because he had once declined to have a vasectomy. It would have been easier and less expensive had he submitted to this rather minor surgical operation, but now he can only regret his earlier inaction.

Betty's case is not an uncommon one, and only those people void of compassion will remain unable to sympathize with her deep and profound disappointment. She simply cannot bring herself to face a future that seems to be a repetition of her previous twenty-three years. Some of her friends in her Sunday School class suggest that she have an abortion at the hospital. But she knows that some other people in the church strongly disapprove. As a committed Christian, she naturally wants to know whether her faith will not only permit an abortion but will support her in her decision if she chooses to have an abortion.

If you were her minister, what passages in the Bible would you turn to in order to help Betty make the right decision? She had made use of birth control measures to prevent pregnancy, but they proved to be imperfect. Must Betty now pay dearly for the imperfections of medical technology? Mark has had a very hard time earning money for his three children. What is he to do now that a fourth child may come into his home? Mark's minister might quote to him the old saying, "Where there's a will, there's a way"; but the minister knows that this is not an infallible biblical proverb and that it does not always hold true. Besides, Betty and Mark honestly have no *will* to raise another child for twenty more years of their lives. Are they to be denounced as uncaring parents?

The evidence shows that far from being uncaring parents, Betty and Mark have gladly made many sacrifices to help make the future of their children more enjoyable and responsible. All that Betty and Mark want now for themselves in their forties is that they, too, be allowed to enjoy their days in a reasonably moderate way. Are they asking for too much? Those people who simply want to be parents *all* their lives (or who even *need* to be parents always) may not be able to understand Betty and Mark. But it would seem to be a part of the Christian morality to learn to understand and appreciate some of the differences among individuals.

Still, abortion is something that Christians have not talked about enough. Is there a Christian case against it? Or is abortion a moral and responsible act, at least in some circumstances? A committed Christian such as Betty Norton has no alternative but to face these questions.

The Case of Irresponsibly Pregnant Women

Susan Cates has already had two abortions. Now she wants a third. My own initial and intemperate reaction to her is this: "Let her carry this third fetus and deliver it. That will teach her that she cannot behave just as she pleases without regard to the consequences!" I can even quote the Old Testament passage, "For they have sown the wind, and they shall reap the whirlwind." (Hosea 8:7 K.J.V.) From the New Testament I can quote, "She that liveth in pleasure is dead while she liveth." (1 Tim. 5:6 K.J.V.)

However, Christians have not been called of God to serve as executioners. History is filled with religious people of all varieties who have decided to take the law of God into their own hands. Against the urging of his all-to-human disciples, Jesus declined to call down fire from heaven upon those Samaritans who had mistreated him. And against one's own intemperate impulses, the Christian would do well to think twice before reacting with punishment against any woman who through carelessness, confusion, stupidity, unchecked lust, or just plain spite has become pregnant without wishing to assume the responsibility of parenthood. Unless Christians think they are wiser than Christ himself, they would do well to consider the parable of the wheat and the tares or weeds. In this parable the servants of the householder, finding weeds growing among the planted wheat, ask for permission to go out immediately and pull up the weeds. But the householder is concerned for his wheat and he thinks that in their zeal the servants will uproot the wheat along with the tares.

Most evangelical Christians have interpreted Christ as saying through this parable that finite and fallible believers cannot proceed on their own to eliminate all the sin in the world without in the process creating a worse situation. Therefore, God will in the end, after the harvest, sort the wheat from the tares. (See Matthew 13:24-30.) In other words, Jesus is reminding his disciples of what they should already have learned from the Old Testament. God says, "Vengeance is mine . . . . for the day of their calamity is at hand." (Deut. 32:35 R.S.V.) The Apostle Paul offers wisdom and caution to his fellow believers:

> *Beloved, never avenge yourselves, but leave it to the wrath of God; for it is written, "Vengeance is mine, I will repay, says the Lord." (Rom. 12:19 R.S.V.)*

Like Christ, Paul recommends overcoming evil with good. (See Romans 12:21.) Again, "Love does no wrong to a neighbor; therefore love is the fulfilling of the law." (Rom. 13:10 R.S.V.)

I would be among the very first to admit that the Christian ideal of overcoming evil with good is not in keeping with our normal worldly way of thinking. We who regard ourselves as the pillars and rocks of the community do not take lightly those persons who become pregnant because they failed to exercise caution and forethought. Our "natural" inclination is to punish them, to teach them a lesson. But there are two things which, if kept in mind, may temper our anger and give us more moral and rational alternatives.

How to Relate to the Irresponsibly Pregnant

In the first place, punishment is not always the only, or even the best, method of teaching people something. Those of us who are parents and spouses know that we often improve the behavior of our children or spouse by an effective use of reward within a context of kindness, respect, good will, and self-respect. Women who become pregnant without concern for their parental responsiblilities may "learn a lesson" much quicker and better if it is learned in a context of Christian compassion, understanding, and steadfast involvement on the part of concerned Christians. It is a slander against Christ for the believer to assume that Christ's preferred method of reform and reconciliation is that of threat and punishment. Speaking "the truth in love," the Christian believer would do well to endeavor to "show . . . a still more excellent way" to those who act irresponsibly and without regard to the social and personal consequences of their sexual behavior.

The second thing that may restrain the Christian's anger against men and women who take pregnancy lightly is the thought of the welfare of the child who will be born in a setting of irresponsibility. If we are concerned for the child's happiness and security, then we will more likely think twice before forcing it to be born into a family that is not ready for it morally and in other significant ways. It may make us *feel* good to know that an irresponsible woman is forced to go pregnant about the neighborhood. "Perhaps the embarrassment and shame will teach her a lesson," we say to ourselves. But in our more constructive and responsible moments we say also, "What kind of life will the child have if it is born of this woman? Does the woman want the child? Is it a *healthy want,* or is the woman using pregnancy simply to satisfy some other need of her own? Is it right to use a child to satisfy her needs? Is it right of us to use a child as an instrument for punishing a wayward or thoughtless woman?" (I will not here speak about the claim that every child is wanted by its mother once it is born, for this whole question of the wanted and unwanted child needs a far more careful analysis than it has received thus far.)

Another point should be brought out regarding our attitude toward irresponsible pregnant women. The Bible teaches that the best of Christian believers are capable of having some evil motives.

Christians, therefore, ought to ask themselves whether in the dark depths of their own lives they are not perhaps harboring a measure of secret envy of the irresponsible woman or man! It is painful sometimes to see that we have motives which are ignoble and for which we need forgiveness. Indeed, a secret envy that is never faced can sometimes lead to resentment, which in turn may fester and lead to the search for a convenient scapegoat. There is nothing in the Christian faith that teaches that Christians are all exempt from motives of envy and resentment. The Bible promises forgiveness and grace. It does not promise sinless perfection among earthly Christians.

The letters of the Apostle Paul make it vividly clear that if angels fell, Christians at least bear watching now and then. These are strong words, but they seem to me to be in harmony with the biblical doctrine of humanity, including the Christian portion of humanity. Every Christian would do well to keep in mind the following statement that Paul himself made regarding his own behavior: "I do not understand my own actions." (Romans 7:15 R.S.V.) We are not fully aware of all our complex motives, and we all realize, now and then at least, that the old Adam is still a part of each of us. This should not cause us to become morbid or enraged that we are imperfect. Rather, it should give us pause, create a greater measure of humility, and cause us to be suspicious of our own urge to punish other people when they fail to act morally and responsibly. To be sure, society has to have certain laws and regulations in order to survive. But the Bible does not give the Christian or anyone else a license to enact as state law every detail of his or her own religion's morality. The state can do only so much in encouraging social responsibility. Beyond a certain point, the state becomes a false god and an object of idolatry.

Of course, abortion may be legal. But is it moral? Some Christians say that abortion is always immoral. Other Christians hold that *not* to have an abortion in some cases is an irresponsible avoidance of one's moral duty. What does the Bible say about abortion?

Abortion and Scripture

The minister, gynecologist, and counselor, R.F.R. Gardner, is surely correct when he writes that on the question of abortion, "there is no clear-cut scriptural guidance."[1] The Christian has no basis for expecting definite *scriptural* guidance unless God has chosen to give it. However, there is some basis for expecting God's *general* revelation outside the Bible to shed light on the question of whether abortion is or is not morally permissible. To be sure, because general revelation does not come already set forth in infallibly written statements, finite human beings must themselves transcribe it into fallible human statements. This means that such statements, while useful and necessary for human living, are nevertheless subject to revision or improvement. All talk among Christians about abortion should, therefore, be carried on in a spirit of humility and with the awareness that no infallible conclusion on abortion has been revealed.

What the Christian may with confidence assert, on the basis of Scripture, is that it is immoral to kill. Or, to be more exact, it is immoral to commit murder. The New English Bible correctly reads, "You shall not commit murder." Of course, every murder is a form of killing, but the Bible distinguishes justified from unjustified killing. Because the latter is clearly murder, it is immoral.

Is Abortion Justified Killing?

But is abortion a case of justified killing? Or, is the abortion of a human fetus a case of killing at all, whether justified or unjustified? Most Christians would agree that abortion is the killing of *something,* but is it the killing of a human *person?* That is the crucial question. Let us suppose that the fetus is in fact a human person. What could possibly justify killing it? Except for strict pacifists, most Christians regard clear self-defense as a justifiable ground for killing. Hence, if the fetus is a serious threat to the life of the mother, then in self-defense she might be justified in having the fetus killed. If a boy twelve years of age should suddenly go strangely berserk to the point of attacking his own mother with a knife, we would tend to say that the mother is justified in killing her berserk son if such is necessary for her self-protection. A fetus that becomes a serious threat to the life of the mother is a bizarre medical case that may call for drastic measures for the mother's own defense and safety.

The Circumstance of Rape

Concerned Christian counselors, gynecologists, ministers, and others are sometimes confronted with cases in which the mother has been a victim of rape! It must be admitted that in most rape cases the fetus cannot in truth be regarded as a threat to the mother's life. To be sure, the conception of the fetus came about without the mother's consent inasmuch as she certainly did not *intend* to have intercourse with her attacker and become pregnant by him. But is that fact a sufficient ground for abortion? Let us assume for the moment that the fetus is indeed a *person.* Then on what authority is the mother justified in killing the fetus simply because she did not intend to have intercourse with her attacker and certainly did not intend to become pregnant?

It is essential to keep in mind that in the case of rape, the mother cannot ordinarily claim self-defense as a basis for abortion. But if she insists that she nevertheless still has a right to kill the fetus-person because she did not intend to have intercourse and become pregnant, then what can be said of another woman who did not *intend* to become pregnant by her *husband* but nevertheless did become pregnant? What I am suggesting here is that in the case of rape, the abortion argument has already shifted from one of the mother's self-defense to one of her personal *consent and intention.*

Those sincere Christians who say that killing a fetus-person is a form of murder are terribly inconsistent when they allow a fetus-person to be killed because the mother was raped. If the fetus is indeed a person when the mother is impregnated by her husband, it is no less a person when the mother is impregnated by someone who has raped her. The evil of the circumstances in which the fetus came about in the womb of a raped mother should not taint the Christian's attitude toward the fetus-person. *If* the fetus is truly a person, then it remains so regardless of the circumstances and conditions of its conception. The resentment against the rapist must not be projected on to the fetus.

But According to Scripture, Is the Fetus a Person?

Of course, the issue of abortion changes considerably if the fetus is not yet a person. The Christian naturally asks, "What does the Bible say about the status of the fetus as a person?" The answer is that the Bible says nothing directly on this question. There is, however, one passage—Exodus 21:22-25—which does suggest indirectly that the fetus is *not* to be regarded as a person. According to this passage, if some men get into a fight and in the process happen to injure a nearby pregnant woman, then the man who injures her will have to pay with his own *life* if the injury proves to be *fatal* to the woman. This is in keeping with the law of "Eye for eye and life for life." If only a member of the woman's body is damaged, then the man will have to pay with the same *member of his own body*. But suppose that the man causes the pregnant woman to have a miscarriage! Obviously, he could not possibly repay with a member of his own body inasmuch as he, being a man, is unable to carry a fetus. What the law of Moses requires of the man in this case is the payment of a *fine*.

It is very significant that the man is *not* required by Hebrew law to pay with his own *life* if the woman's fetus is killed by him. This suggests, therefore, that unlike the woman, the fetus is not yet considered to be a human person. To this day, many Jewish believers hold that the fetus does not become a person until the normal time of birth. While there is no direct Old Testament basis for this precise position, it is at least not in conflict with the Old Testament. According to the New Testament, the babe in the womb of Elizabeth "leaped." It was Elizabeth who *interpreted* this fetal activity as a leap "for joy." (Luke 1:44) Evangelical Christians need not regard Elizabeth's *interpretation* to be divine revelation. The inspired Luke himself says only that "the babe leaped in her womb." (1:41)

What Does General Revelation Say
About the Status of the Fetus?

Since the Bible offers no direct information regarding whether a fetus is or is not a person, the Christian has no alternative other than to turn to God's general revelation outside the Bible. What, then, do medical research, biological inquiry, and other "life sciences" indicate? Those involved in fetal research have pointed out that the fetus *in utero* is found to be sensitive to certain stimuli and that it even emits brain waves of its own. It is alive and has certain traits unique to it.

Some lay people have jumped from this fact to the conclusion that the fetus must be classified as an actual person. But this conclusion overlooks the challenging fact that many other creatures—from horses to cats—emit their own distinctive brain waves. Indeed, the brain waves of these creatures are even more vital and complex than those of the human fetus. Furthermore, the brains of most living animals are far more sensitive to a greater range of stimuli than are the brains of newly born human infants. Therefore, if the complex and vital brain states of these living animals cannot qualify these animals as actual persons, then neither can the rather modest brain states of the human fetus qualify it as an actual person.

One of the leading brain physiologists in America, Dr. Jose M.R. Delgado, writes of the human infant:

> In summary, it is unlikely that before the moment of birth the baby has any significant visual, auditory, olfactory, or gustatory experiences, and it is probable that it has received only a very limited amount of tacticle, organic, and proprioceptive information . . . In an experimental study of seventeen behavioral responses, their intercorrelations proved to be zero, indicating that "there is no mental integration in the newborn child."[2]

Dr. Delgado goes on to say that if the fetus has awareness at all, it is a meager awareness at best that cannot be regarded as comparable to consciousness in children and adults. What should be pointed out here is that the human infant is quite special in that he or she must be nourished and developed at length in *two* wombs—that of the mother and that of the family and community in which the newborn infant "grows up." Again I quote Dr. Delgado: "The newborn brain is not capable of speech, symbolic understanding, or of directing skillful motility."[3] All such developments will usually come about gradually as the infant spends many more months being nourished and stimulated inside the second womb (i.e., the social womb of family or community). "We must conclude," says Dr. Delgado, "that there are no detectable signs of mental activity at birth and *that human beings are born without minds.*"[4]

This is not to say that the infant is without *potential* for eventually developing a mind or mindful activity as a responsible moral agent. But potentiality should not be confused with reality. A block of marble is not yet a great piece of inspiring sculpture. It is only potentially so. A sperm cell or an ovum is only *potentially* a human being, but not *actually* so. A human fetus is potentially a human person, but not actually so. "Experimental studies show that the reactions of newborn babies are so elemental that they can hardly be considered signs of a functioning mind."[5] Furthermore, "the term 'emotion' should not be ascribed to infant behavior because it lacks differentiated responses."[6]

As most mothers realize, the labor of childbirth is only half the job. The remaining part of their job as a parent is to help nurture and nourish the infant in countless ways so that it may eventually become a developed human person. No other creatures on earth equal human parents in responsibility in caring for their young. Human infants, in comparison with other creatures, are at birth so anatomically and physiologically undeveloped as to require a long postnatal growing period.

Human beings are born with such cerebral immaturity that their very survival depends completely on exterior help, and their behavior is similar to that of a purely spinal being, or at most, of a brain stem or midbrain preparation. Most neurologists agree that the neonate is a noncortical being. After birth, there is a transitional period during which the cerebral cortex starts to function, and then its activities progressively increase until a reciprocal functional correlation is established with the rest of the brain.[7]

Dr. Peter Nathan, research neurologist at London's National Hospital for Nervous Diseases, points out how utterly crucial the "social stimulation" is to the infants's development.[8] This is not to underestimate the remarkable brain of the human infant but rather to say that this brain requires additional social intake just as the infant's body as a whole requires the intake of food if it is to develop and grow. Indeed, it is no exaggeration to say that without the extracerebral factors that come about through living in the social womb of family or the community, the human brain would never begin to function as a mind.

It may come as a surprise to some sincere Christians to realize that there is no scriptural basis for thinking that God has chosen to take normally no more than nine months after conception in which to bring a human *person* into existence. The evidence from *general* revelation strongly indicates that it takes many more than nine months before a human person finally comes into being. This conclusion may be contrary to certain old wives' tales. the tradition of the elders, or simply uninformed assumptions. But the Christian is bound neither morally nor religiously to worship at these hoary shrines. They are not a legitimate part of the faith. If the general revelation of God guides in a direction opposite that of old tales, assumptions and traditions, then the Christian is committed to following the light that general revelation provides.

The Christian is free to follow the suggestions of general revelation so long as they do not clearly run counter to the explicit teachings revealed in the special revelation of sacred Scripture. Indeed, it may be said that his or her commitment is to give greater weight to the leads of general revelation than to the unchallenged opinions of antiquity. After all, Christianity owes its allegiance to neither ancestor worship nor the adoption of every novel fad that comes along. The steady research into the status of the fetus indicates strongly that the fetus is not yet a person. Therefore, the commandment against unjustified killing or murder does not apply to it. Abortion is certainly not a very wise method of birth control, but it is not a case of murder or homicide.

Is the IUD a Tool of Abortion?

Those who insist that abortion is murder are faced with the problem of the intrauterine contraceptive device (IUD). The IUD appears to work after fertilization but before implantation.[9] If inside the mother a human *person* comes into being at the time of fertilization, then the IUD is in effect a tool of murder. If I sincerely believed that the human person comes into being at the time of fertilization, I would certainly seek to ban the use of the IUD. From my perspective, the murder of human persons should always be made illegal. Some of my private morality I do not seek to translate into laws of the state. But when it comes to murder of human persons, then I am definitely not content to say, "Well, because some people think murder is all right, I will not press for legislation against murder." I want murder to be legislated against. And if the use of the IUD brings about the direct murder of persons, then the IUD should certainly be outlawed. Whatever one's *moral* view on adultery may be, I do not think adultery should be against the law of the *state,* for it is an act between two willing adults. But in the case of murder, it is normally not a transaction involving a positive preference on the part of the victim.

However, I must say clearly as possible that I have found no good reason to believe that a human *person* comes into being at the time that the male's sperm fertilizes the female's ovum. And that is one reason why I do not oppose the sale and use of the IUD. A Roman Catholic, Professor Vincent C. Punzo argues at length that a human person does come into existence as soon as the egg is fertilized by the sperm cell. But he does not deal with the problem of the IUD, although he seems not to be opposed to birth control devices short of abortion. Unfortunately, if Professor Punzo were consistent with his own position, he would have to conclude that the IUD is an instrument of abortion and therefore is, in his view, a weapon for committing murder.

Professor Punzo does acknowledge that "at least 38 per cent of all zygotes [i.e., fertilized human eggs] are spontaneously aborted."[10] But he does not accuse God of murder in these cases. He seems, rather, to accept morally these spontaneous abortions on the ground that the fetuses that are aborted by miscarriage "are usually defective."

But this opens wide the door for Christians to discuss whether it is morally permissible to *induce* the abortion of a fetus that is judged by critical medical opinion to be a defective fetus. It has been claimed that if God does not cause a miscarriage of a particular defective fetus, then God actually *wanted* it to be born. But this kind of second-guessing of God's wishes has all sorts of cruel implications. It used to be said by many Christians that God did not want women to have the benefit of any anesthesia during the time of their giving birth to their infants. Today, however, Christians are not so eager to believe that physicians should refrain from helping women in their time of labor pain. Indeed, some physicians and others are teaching women how to reduce labor pain by methods other than anesthesia. Incidentally, Adam was told that he would in the *sweat* of his face eat his bread, but few Christians think that this announcement rules out air conditioning units and fans for people.

Family members sometimes divide sharply on how to relate personally to someone in the family, or to some close friend of the family, who has had an abortion. There is little doubt that the healing of this division would be made more likely if there could be agreement on the question of whether the fetus is a person. What we believe certainly does affect what we feel and how we react to ourselves and others. In this chapter, I have been working on the assumption that nothing reinforces a reasonable mind better than a case set forth in a reasonable and forthright manner. I have tried thus far to show why the view that the fetus is not a person is in harmony with both Scripture and general revelation. Anxiety, depression, and hard feelings among family members and friends is often brought about by conflicting beliefs. That is why in this chapter I have regarded it as very practical to deal with beliefs about the status of the fetus. I wish now to proceed further along this avenue of thought.

The Entrance of the Soul

According to believers of various religious traditions, the human soul enters or unites with the human fetus long before the fetus is born. And this fact, they claim, is what makes the fetus in the mother an *actual person* distinct from the mother. Unfortunately, as one leading evangelical Christian theologian notes, this entire question of the origin of the soul is cloaked in mystery and is at best a matter of precarious speculation.[11] Speaking of the origin of the soul, one theologian writes, "Direct biblical evidence is non-existent . . . . "[12] Evangelicals in particular seem to prefer the Traducian theory of the origin of the soul, wherein both the soul and the body are inherited from the parents. One advantage that this theory is said to provide is that it does not require each soul to be created from nothing. Rather, each soul comes into existence through "natural generation." God is said to work now "in general through the law and processes of nature."[13]

It would seem that this Traducian theory has a second advantage, namely, that it opens the door to the possibility of a scientific study of the origin and development of the soul. Unfortunately, in the words of one scholar, "Modern studies in heredity and psychosomatic unity are indecisive . . . . "[14]

Even when we follow some theologians in concluding that the soul is "produced by natural generation" and comes from the parents, we still have no basis for asserting that the soul develops in the fetus before rather than after the birth of the fetus. In fact, Christians would be less than candid if they should try to deny that they need to learn to speak much more intelligibly about the characteristics and activities of the soul if they are going to use it to throw light on the current discussions on abortion and the status of the fetus. Theologians still differ as to whether the hu-

man soul and spirit are identical or distinguishable realities.[15]
There are many theories of the soul, some of which are said to
be Christian but which are perhaps more closely related to the
theories of Plato or other ancients. The Bible does not set forth
a systematic doctrine of the soul. According to Psalm 107:5, the
soul can hunger and thirst. According to Revelation 6:9, the
writer claims to have seen in his vision only the souls, not the
bodies, of "those who had been slain." Apparently, souls can
be "seen," can suffer hunger and thirst, but cannot bleed or
cease to exist altogether. My purpose here, however, is not to
venture into a systematic study of the concept of "soul" as represented throughout the Bible, but rather to indicate that Christians cannot on biblical grounds conclude either that the human
soul is sufficient to make a human fetus into a *person* or that
the soul comes into being before the mother gives birth to the
fetus. Mark C. Cambron insists that the Bible asserts that even
animals have souls.[16]

Habit may lead us to continue to think that only persons
can have souls, but habit is not a source of infallible divine revelation. The Christian may leave open the possibility that there
exist souls of certain heavenly creatures which are not persons.
At least some of the angels are described in ways that suggest
that they are souls, yet the Christian believer is raised above
them in rank and is the recipient of their ministry and service.
(See Hebrews 1:14.) Indeed, the Apostle Paul says that Christians
will finally judge the angels. (1 Cor. 6:3) Yet in his humiliation,
Christ was said to be made a little lower than the angels. (See
Hebrews 2:9.) But it is not clear in what respect he was lower.

The angels are called "ministering spirits," (see Hebrews
1:14) and often in the Bible the terms "spirit" and "soul" have
the same meaning, although not always. The seraphim and cheru-
bim do not appear to be persons, although they do seem to be
souls in heaven. But this is inconclusive. In summary, we may
say that no theory of the soul is sufficiently developed to allow
us to draw any conclusions about the status of the fetus by referring to the doctrine of the soul.

Distinguishing Mark of Personhood

In recent decades Christians have begun to raise the question among themselves as to whether there are persons on other planets who need to receive the gospel of Christ. Of course, there already exist various kinds of life on earth that are not given the message of Christ for the simple reason that they are not regarded as persons. No one thinks to convert a gorilla to Christianity. But suppose that someday on another planet we should meet some gorilla-looking creatures that seem to be *more* than a gorilla. Surely, we cannot refuse to give the title of "personhood" to someone merely because he or she *looks* like a gorilla. If certain creatures on another planet should cause us to pause and raise the question "Are they actual persons?" then they must have manifested some characteristic that distinguishes them from gorillas and that makes us feel them to be very much like ourselves. Indeed, if they are very much like us, we may set up a moral rule prohibiting the enslavement of these creatures or prohibiting our making them into food for ourselves.

The only way we have of determining whether to classify any creature as a person is to observe *how it acts, responds, and behaves.* If we notice that the members of a certain group of creatures seem to have a *developed and elaborate language* which they use in communicating with one another, we will more likely think of them as persons. (Of course we must not insist that it be our sort of language. There are many ways to communicate.) It is quite significant that according to the book of Genesis, one of the first things that Adam did was to give a name to every living creature (or every class of living creatures). Nothing is said of these creatures giving Adam a name. (See Genesis 2:19-20.) One reason that Christians have regarded the serpent in the Garden of Eden as really Satan in disguise is that the serpent carried on a conversation with Eve. No lower animal could do that. So, we tend to say that being able to converse in a language of some sort in an elaborate manner is one thing that separates persons from other creatures. Gorillas do not compose poems. Dogs and horses can no more create proverbs and oral traditions than cats and zebras can experiment elaborately with mathematical symbols.

If we observe the human fetus' actions and responses, we may have to say that it is much closer to a zebra than to a person. At the same time, while it is inaccurate to classify a fetus as an actual person, the fetus is something that the zebra could not possibly be. It is a *potential* person. To be a potential anything is to say that it will eventually become that thing *if* it receives the proper conditions. A zebra simply cannot become a person no matter what additional conditions it is supplied with. A human female's egg is altogether different from the zebra in one crucial respect—the *unfertilized egg is a potential person.* And if that egg is supplied with the proper conditions—including a fertilizing sperm cell as well as a nourishing blood supply—then eventually, if all goes well, the egg will *become* a human person. It is true that the average woman loses 30,000 eggs in her lifetime. Each of these eggs is a potential person, but we do not regard women as agents of mass murder. Nor do we say that each woman justifiably killed 30,000 persons, for the eggs were only *potentially,* not actually, persons. The same may be said of the fetus, only we must add that the fetus has a much greater potential for eventually becoming a person because it has received a supply of proper conditions that help make actual personhood become a reality in the course of many months.

Nevertheless, the fetus cannot be taught to manipulate symbols in an elaborate manner. It lacks the potential for that kind of behavior. But it does have the kind of potential to take on eventually new potentials of the kind that will make language or the elaborate manipulation of symbols an actuality. The fetus is a *genuinely potential* person, whereas the zebra is not. That is precisely why, if a woman decides not to have an abortion, she then places herself under a new moral obligation to take good care of her fetus. The way she cares for it now will determine to some extent the kind of person it will actually become in due time. We certainly do not want her to damage the tiny brain of the fetus because such a damage might affect the person that will someday develop from that fetus. I would go so far as to say that if a woman is not going to take good care of her fetus, then it is better that she have an abortion.

Other Marks of Personhood

We have seen that using an elaborate language is a distinguishing mark of personhood. In the book of Genesis, God is represented as talking with Adam and Eve but not with birds or cattle. To be sure, animals and birds do communicate somewhat with one another, but they do not have the capacity for the elaborate *descriptive* language that we have. Nor do they enjoy the *explanatory* dimensions of language and symbols that we enjoy. We share with other animals an *expressive* language, but even our powers of expression—in poetry, art, music, etc.— far excel even the brightest bird or beast of the field.

If on another planet we should meet creatures who, while not physically resembling ourselves, were nevertheless gifted in descriptive, expressive, and explanatory responses, then we would tend to regard them as persons. (White men entering Africa often failed to see black men and women *as persons* because in part these white men failed to observe how very complex and elaborate the languages of the Africans were.)

Following on the heels of an elaborate language is the powerful activity known as complex reasoning and thinking, including abstract thinking. Because we can use symbols to represent things—whether real or imaginary—we have an enormous advantage over horses, dogs, deer, etc. It is profoundly significant that in the Bible the word of God never comes *to* animals, even though on rare occasions it may come *through* them. Animals have knowledge and know-how, and they can even communicate some of this know-how to their offspring. But the power of communication among ourselves is incomparably greater than that among elephants and tigers. Furthermore, *we communicate about very many things and about things existing under all sorts of conditions and in all sorts of relationships.* Because this is the case, we are able to engage in moral discourse and complex evaluations. We speculate and experiment in our imaginations and learn to test out our speculations in the observable world. Most animals speculate a bit, but compared to ourselves they are thoroughly retarded and painfully slow in most areas of what we call "learning."

The Bible speaks often of "the word of God." This might better be translated to read "the *communication* of God." But there is no record at all of God as having communicated his message to a fetus. And the reason for this is simple. The fetus could not have understood the message. The heavens do not declare the glory of God to a fetus because it still lacks the potential for learning directly the concepts either of the heavens or of God's glory. The fetus can make only comparatively negligible responses, most of which are less vital and complex than the responses of a newborn colt. The Christian seems led to conclude that God has seen fit to develop most animals to a high level of appropriate maturity inside their mothers, whereas in the case of human beings *God seems to have given fathers and other members of the community, as well as mothers, the opportunity and responsibility of helping slowly to transform the human fetus into a human person.*

In short, personhood develops only through *interpersonal communication.* I suggest that herein lies the image of God in man and woman. God as Father, Son, and Holy Spirit is the supreme interpersonal communication; the human family or community is the finite reflection of this divine image. The fetus is not a person, for it has not yet entered into the second womb—the community womb of interpersonal communication. When the infant begins to participate in the community and to develop the powers of communication to a degree and range of elaboration that exceeds that of non-personal animals, then it *becomes a person.* There is nothing magical about this process. Through natural and social processes (which the Christian regards as divinity ordained) the human infant develops to the point that it begins to function and behave as a person and therefore becomes a person. To *be* a person is to *respond and act* as a person.

The Rise of Conscience

In keeping with what can be learned through general revelation in connection with Scripture, the Christian can see that the fetus does not develop a personal conscience inside the mother's womb. Rather, certain potentials are developed there. After birth and over a period of months and years the womb of community and family nourishes the helpless infant until slowly and sometimes painfully the child develops a conscience, a sensitivity to moral regulations, and a compassion for others. A fetus knows little of compassion for others or of moral imperatives, for such profound developments are characteristics and marks of *persons*. The fetus needs normally nine months to develop before it can enter the second womb, where it will again require many more months to grow and be cared for until it develops those unique and special characteristics of personhood.

The Question of Infanticide

If it takes many months, or perhaps even a year or two, before the infant begins to show steady signs of personhood, then is the Christian ever justified in taking the life of an *infant* that has already been born into its family and community? If a two-week old infant is not yet a person, then may a Christian mother ask that it be put to death if she learns that it is, say, an incurable hydrocephalic? I have a friend whose last child is a basket case. It neither speaks nor acts in a way that a person would be expected to act. Indeed, it is less active than the average week-old kitten. The parents now have their infant in an institution where the state pays for most of its care. I know of no biblical teaching that would require these parents to keep the infant at home so that they might watch after it day after day. In biblical time, many malformed infants would have died within a very short period of time, whereas today's modern medical advances make it possible to keep seriously malformed infants alive for years. Because of medical and technological changes in our modern situations, we need a morality that is sensitive to such changes. Some moral principles abide, but additional moral rules and guidelines are sometimes needed to deal with new circumstances and conditions.

Dale Evans has written movingly of how a retarded child became a blessing to her. But there are degrees of retardation.

My friend received comparatively little response from his hydrocephalic infant; certainly no *personal* responses have been forthcoming. Of course, Dale Evans and Roy Rogers, with their enormous bank account, are able to pay for extraordinary services and for someone to come into their home to help them with their parental responsibilities. But my friend whose offspring is hydrocephalic is a busy minister, whose income is not even in the shadow of that of Dale Evans and Roy Rogers. It is perhaps even unfair to compare these two cases.

With reluctance I conclude that in light of certain real tragedies in the lives of some families, Christians ought to face courageously and humbly the possibility that in some cases it is moral to take the life of a seriously retarded infant. There is nothing Christian about making moral decisions from indiscriminate and blind emotion, just as there is nothing particularly Christian about making moral decisions void of emotion. I am not altogether sure that I would support even carefully controlled infanticide, but I do think that Christians are now obligated to give this alternative long and careful attention and discriminating discussion. It may be that some Christians who have the financial means to pay for aids and helpers to come into their homes to help raise a seriously retarded infant will *volunteer to adopt the retarded.*

I can find no firm basis for concluding that a woman's decision to have an abortion is a serious moral problem at all, inasmuch as the fetus is not a person. But even though I regard a newborn infant to be not yet a person, I would prefer to hear much more careful and informed debate before the selective killing of the seriously and hopelessly retarded infants is regarded as no longer a critical moral problem.

A normal infant is much closer to personhood than a fetus is; and the closer it comes to personhood, the more care and caution is needed in any talk of the taking of life. I think that a society is insensitive, cruel, and immoral when it requires a husband and wife to care for, say, a hydrocephalic infant. The moral thing, at least, would be for some section of the community to come to the parents' rescue. *How* it comes to the rescue is something that concerned Christians need to explore in practical detail. The Bible speaks of bearing the burdens of one another. Unfortunately, under the mistaken notion that some of our traditional ways are God's ways, sincere Christians sometimes add on to the backs of their fellow men and women burdens so heavy as to make life excessively harsh and repressive. But this need not be the case, which is one reason for my writing this particular chapter.

Abortion and Feelings of Guilt

Christian missionaries frequently discover that recent converts to the Christian faith are suffering from strong *feelings of guilt* because they have given up the religion and certain customs of their ancestors and family. The missionaries do not conclude, however, that the new converts should therefore go back to their old ways just because of these guilt-feelings. Rather, they try to show the new converts that their guilt-feelings, while understandable, are not *justified*. With considerable skill, some missionaries draw in the minds of the new converts a sharp line between *real* guilt, on the one hand, and guilt-*feelings,* on the other hand. The hope is that as the converts see that they are *not really guilty of something just because they have converted to Christianity,* they will in time cease altogether to experience the *feeling* of guilt.

I do not think there is usually any *real guilt* in having an abortion, although there may indeed be real guilt involved in not taking appropriate precautions for preventing pregnancy in the first place. The fact that a person may *feel* guilty about an abortion does not mean that the *abortion itself* is in fact morally wrong. A Christian friend and counselor can be of considerable help to women who feel guilty about their abortion. They can be led to see that in the given circumstances, the abortion may have been the right course of action to take.

If there is any real guilt because of the way that the woman became pregnant, then the Christian may deal with this actual guilt in terms of repentance and forgiveness. To say, therefore, that an abortion is wrong because the woman might suffer guilt feelings is to place the cart before the horse. The primary issue has to do with whether the abortion is morally permitted or even morally required. The guilt *feelings* that might follow an abortion are phenomena that the understanding Christian might wish to help control or even eliminate. Instead of being like Job's comfortless comforters, Christians would do well to become a genuine comfort to women who upon having an abortion are suffering *unjustified feelings* of guilt.

The Impact of Abortion on the Husband

Jeff Weil met Norma Ryan at the church where both were members. By a previous marriage, Norma had given birth to two children whom she now had the responsibility of caring for. Eventually Jeff, who had never been married, came to love Norma very much, and she in turn came to love him. Jeff knew that he would be taking on an enormous responsibility if he should someday ask Norma to marry him, but he concluded that he wanted very much to be her husband. The new marriage progressed quite well for about a year. The couple moved to another town and immediately became active in one of the churches in the town. Another year elapsed when Norma was told by her doctor that she was pregnant.

But the news came as no surprise to her, for she and Jeff had talked about having a child of their own. In time, however, Norma began to have serious second thoughts, especially as Jeff began to drink considerably. To make the story short, Norma could no longer, at the age of forty, look forward to raising a new child. She was herself working at a full-time job. Knowing full well that she had willingly agreed to become pregnant, she now came to regret that she had made this decision.

Jeff, however, wanted very much a child of his own, and the very thought of his wife's contemplating an abortion angered him exceedingly. Norma, on the other hand, reasoned that Jeff's drinking problem was something that she did not want to inflict on a newborn child. Finally, she decided that her initial agreement to become pregnant was sincere but one which should never have been made. She asked her physician to give her an abortion, which, after counseling with her at length, he proceeded to do.

Jeff continued to drink considerably and eventually was forced to resign his job because he had been given a ticket for driving while under the influence of alcohol.

There are other cases, however, in which the husband seems to be much more responsible than Jeff but whose wife nevertheless wants an abortion despite her husband's wishes to the contrary. The hostility that builds up between husband and wife in this kind of situation is sometimes almost more than the couple can bear. Yet, if the marriage is to be meaningful to both of them, some means of reconciliation has to be found.

It is a bit too easy to say that each spouse should forgive the other in this case, for neither person thinks that he or she has done wrong under the circumstances. Sometimes Christians are too eager to turn a case of complexity into a case of evil motives. It is important to see that often life is tragic and complicated and that there is no biblical ground for supposing that every issue is a moral issue. For example, John wants very much to marry his fiancee, Elizabeth, who has been going with him for four years. Their friends agree that they would make an ideal married couple, and their minister would be very pleased to perform the marriage ceremony.

But there is a serious problem and they need their minister's help. John's mother is an invalid. She is also "bossy," so much so that John and Elizabeth agree that it would not be good for their marriage if John's mother should live with them. The problem, then, can be stated in this way: should John leave his mother and marry Elizabeth? His mother thinks that in her special circumstances, she very much needs John, her only son, to remain at home with her.

The minister felt it necessary to point out that John's problem was not one of good motives versus evil motives. In both cases, his motivation was very good. Similarly, when husband and wife differ on the question of her having an abortion, their difference may not be one of wholly good versus wholly evil motives. Instead, the difference may be one of divergent *beliefs*. If Henry believes that the fetus is a person, he cannot help concluding that his wife Virginia is committing murder by having an abortion. Virginia, on the other hand, believing that her decision is a moral one, feels that she would be failing to exercise her God-given intelligence and moral agency if she should give birth to this fetus in this circumstance.

What can be done to reconcile this husband and wife? There is no easy answer. If you were Henry, could you respect a woman—even your wife—if you thought that she had willingly participated in a murder? You might, *if* she should acknowledge her sin, repent, and seek forgiveness. But in this case, Virginia has the conviction that the abortion, far from an act of murder, is an act of moral responsibility. In her mind, she should not confess as a sin something which is a moral act. There are in fact couples who disagree sharply about whether abortion is or is not a case of unjustified homicide. That is why it may be necessary for the couple to relate to each other on the level of discussing their *beliefs.* That is, it is not, first of all, a question of whether one is or is not going to forgive the other. Rather it is a question of opening up the lines of communication and information so that there will be the possibility of one spouse's changing his or her belief by looking at the evidence from Scripture and general revelation. In this chapter, I have endeavored openly to present reasons why we may conclude that because the fetus is not yet a person, abortion is not murder.

When Irrational Guilt Strikes

There is of course enormous social pressure against both abortion and masturbation. Sometimes the pressure is so powerful that even the strongest Christian has difficulty resisting it even though believing in his or her mind and heart that neither masturbation nor abortion is wrong per se. But what is this person to do when, despite convictions but because of social pressure, he or she still *feels* guilty? I have already discussed the importance of separating the *psychological feeling* of guilt from *real* guilt. But now I think it will be of practical use to show very briefly how a Christian can actually strengthen well-grounded convictions against the intimidations of social pressure.

First, one must set up plans to talk with a minister or

others who also hold to the position that abortion (or masturbation) may be right and proper for Christians. Because no person is a self-contained unit, each individual must have encouragement from other people to develop and retain personal beliefs and convictions. There is a time to have one's beliefs challenged and critically evaluated. There is even a time to change or modify one's beliefs for good and sound reasons. But there is also a time when a person needs to be *encouraged by others to hold fast to beliefs* in the face of social pressure. Beliefs should not submit to unreasonable and unsupported pressure from other people.

Normally, individuals find it very difficult to do what they think is right if those whom they respect tell them that they do not support them in their endeavor. It is important that a woman who has experienced an abortion not wait until friends or relatives approach her to offer their support. She would do well to look around and pick out those trustworthy persons who would offer her strong support. Then she should go to one of those trustworthy persons for words of encouragement.

If the husband and wife are in agreement on the abortion, they owe it to themselves to sit down a number of times to express to one another their sense of satisfaction in having made a moral and rational decision. If spouses have a difficult time talking with one another on this matter, then a minister, physician, or psychotherapist might be an excellent "reinforcement environment" so long as they agree that abortion is not wrong per se.

Also, there are some very understanding friends inside one's church or town that may prove to be effective in giving moral support in crises. We do well to remember to turn to those whose friendship has been tested and proved trustworthy. In addition, the Christian must not forget to ask for divine help to carry on after having made the decision to have an abortion. It is useful to write oneself notes: phone a friend, see the minister, remember to pray for divine help.

Another step can be taken when ungrounded guilt strikes. Often it is quite effective to confront *ungrounded* guilt with *real* guilt. For example, in the case of abortion, the Christian may train herself to *judge* as contrary to Christian morality the tendency to give in to ungrounded feelings of guilt. In other words, flashes of unjustified guilt must be treated as we treat other irrational whims or impulses. They must be seen as temptations to be ignored, laughed at, or treated in whatever way proves to be the most effective method of controlling them.

Irrational and unjustified feelings of guilt can be better handled if Christian men and women can see them for what they really are, namely, a hindrance to effective Christian living. Flashes of unjustified feelings of guilt may best be compared to flashes of unjustified feelings of anger. They interfere with responsible behavior. To be sure, there are times when we should feel anger—when such a feeling is justified and is useful in carrying out responsible tasks. Similarly, there are times when we should have guilt feelings—when they are justified and useful for carrying out responsibilities. But when flashes of guilt feelings regarding abortion hit the Christian, she must not hesitate to tell herself that these feelings are a hindrance to effective and vital Christian living. Indeed, if she is convinced that abortion is not murder, then she would do well to *practice* telling herself that it is her responsibility as a Christian to keep ungrounded guilt feelings about abortion from interfering with her life. She may not be able to prevent these feelings from appearing in her mind now and then but she can determine that with the help of Christ she will not allow them to be regarded as more than a kind of irritation that may have to be endured for only a season.

Finally, to any Christian considering a past or future abortion, I would recommend that she copy down the following and place it in a very handy place—in her purse, for instance.

Because parenthood is a God-given privilege and not simply a state to slip into mindlessly, I will convenant with God to give birth only to those children whom I have a strong desire to bring into this world and whom I can love in a practical, concrete, and effective way. Furthermore, if I cannot wholeheartedly give birth to a fetus, I will have an abortion rather than submit to the group pressures to give birth to the fetus against my convictions.

_____
Signed

Sensitivity to Human Life

It has been charged that abortion is a part of the modern disregard for human life. Most of those who make this charge hold that the fetus is a person. Needless to say, if I held to this view of the fetus, I, too, would certainly regard abortion as insensitive barbarism. But civil and civilized living requires us to make important and crucial distinctions and discriminations, which is what I have tried to do in this chapter on the issue of the status of the fetus. I, along with many others, am deeply concerned that the commitment to the value of persons not be spread too thin and indiscriminately. True, this is a rather conservative position for me to take, but I think it justified in this case. Radicals on the issue of abortion such as James and William F. Buckley are appalled at the thought that a fetus will not be classified as a person. Yet these same two men seem to me to be much too insensitive to the needs and sorrows of great numbers of human children and parents who are already clearly persons. Why would someone become alarmed about the fate of a fetus and then appear rather smug about the living conditions of certain ten-year old children? Why would an outspoken preacher remain perfectly silent on Richard Nixon's renewed bombing of Hanoi in 1972 and yet speak out boldly against abortion? [17] I look forward to the day when those who get worked up about the right of the fetus to be given birth will get worked up even more over the fact that many of our old people are filed away in those kinds of "rest homes" that are hardly more than institutions for transforming a person steadily into a non-person. I regard myself as a true conservative in calling for the careful conservation of the lives of those human persons who already have been born into the world of personhood. Besides, while the Bible is silent about the status of the fetus, it is far from silent about the duty of children to their parents. Seeing to it that the aged are well cared for would seem to be a practical application of the commandment to honor one's parents.

Treating a fetus as if it were a person is misplaced responsibility. To be sure, if a woman is committed to bringing her fetus into personhood, *then* both she and society are morally bound to care dearly for the health of that fetus. But *if* the woman's decision is to have an abortion, *then* Christians must think of helping the woman and other real persons involved in the decision.

Himself a committed and conservative Christian, the gynecologist Dr. R.F.R. Gardner thinks that the following quotation is unfortunately true: " 'Conservative Christian opponents of abortion . . . speak vividly of the alternatives conceivably open to a woman but do all too little to press for those reforms which will make the alternative actually available.' "[18] Recently, however, a new social concern among some younger spokespersons has begun to materialize. Richard Quebedeaux in his forthright book *The Young Evangelicals* contends that his own conservative Christian theology need not be bound by traditions and assumptions which, while passing as biblical, are upon closer examination seen to be not biblical at all. It is my hope that this serious-minded movement of the "young evangelicals" will take a fresh look at the question of abortion. I think that some of those of this movement will agree with me that traditional, conservative Christian reaction against abortion was not biblically based. What *is* biblically based, however, is the imperative to help ease the burdens of those women who are facing difficult moral decisions and are asking for help. "Blessed *are* the merciful: for they shall obtain mercy." (Matt. 5:7 K.J.V.)

IV
WHEN CHRISTIANS DIVORCE

Clergymen and Divorce

The title of this chapter is "*When* Christians Divorce," rather than "*Should* Christians Divorce?" Some of the more conservative Christians have always been aware that divorce is not a part of the divine ideal of marriage. It has come as a shock to them to learn that the chilling frost of divorce has begun to fall upon their marriages. Some Christians look upon divorce as something which unbelievers indulge in but which they themselves will never fall victim to. But the Apostle Paul was concerned that, after having preached the gospel for many years, he might himself fail to measure up in Christian living. Christians today cannot afford to be less concerned about their own pattern of Christian living. Aaron Livingston and Eric Daniels, two dedicated Protestant ministers, had devoted themselves to their Christian calling for over two decades. But each was wholly unprepared for the shattering experience of watching his wife walk out of his life to seek a divorce. I will return to discuss these two men after making a few preparatory comments.

We often hear it said that if Christ is in our hearts, then divorce will never enter our homes. But this way of speaking offends the consciences of many Christians, not because they disbelieve it, but because it and similar statements are often uttered too lightly. To turn a significant statement into a cliché or religious commercial is a serious offense in the minds of many Christians. Indeed, the commandment that prohibits taking the name of the Lord in vain is best rendered as follows: "Do not take up the name of the Lord lightly." Taking Christ into one's heart in the full sense of the statement is not something that can be compared to yoga breathing or Transcendental Meditation. Nor is taking Christ into one's life to be compared to taking an aspirin tablet into one's stomach. When Paul tells the believer to take on the mind of Christ, he is not talking about one simple exercise or experience but a rich and multicolored *way of life* that the believer takes on daily and over a period of years. In the case of Christian married couples, taking on the mind of Christ may include the actual practice of nourishing their marital relationship daily. This means that they will sometimes need to be alert to better ways of enriching their marriage, just as a horticulturist will be alert to new information and new methods for cultivating plants. It is misleading to think that taking Christ into one's heart is something different from actually living the Christian life. Some people give the erroneous impression that receiving Christ in the heart is a spooky experience, as if the believer were having a "seance with Jesus."

Christian marriages may be in for more strain and trouble than we have hitherto imagined. And that is why it remains imperative to equip the Christian with more than words of piety or mere talk of Christ in the heart. Clichés, even when composed of Christian-sounding words, have little influence in bracing believers, against the winds and torrents that come upon them in their pilgrims' progress. The real question for Christians, then, is not *whether* they must have Christ in their hearts in order to maintain a good Christian marriage in the face of much opposition. Rather the question has to do with *how* they go about realizing more fully the presence of Christ in their life or marriage.

Christ taught that his followers must learn to be as wise as serpents. How does a Christian become wise, at least sufficiently wise to live the victorious Christian life? One way to start is by observing and listening. There is a time to open one's mouth to preach and proclaim what one knows and believes. And there is also a time to open one's eyes, ears, and mind in order to learn how to cope in the world in a Christian way. Christ promised that we should find if we but seek. But there is no promise of finding without seeking in places that we may never before have thought to look.

For example, we see divorces taking place all about us. We also see that some groups are not divorcing very much. Instead of pretending that we already know why some groups are successful in standing against divorce, we would do well to observe and learn. Take the Mormons, whose rate of divorce is very low. Seeking to find out why the Mormons are successful in controlling divorce, we soon learn that it definitely is *not* because of their orthodox Christian beliefs, for their beliefs about God, Christ, sin, salvation, faith, etc. are far removed from orthodox Christian beliefs. But if the cause for the low rate of divorce among Mormons is not their religious doctrines, what is it? Christians who are concerned about the threat of divorce in their own churches would do well to learn whatever they can from Mormons and any other group that offers some insight into the problem. With some surprise, I came to the conclusion that the low divorce rate among Mormons has nothing of significance to do with their theological doctrines. We still have much to learn about the numerous conditions that make possible a stable, meaningful, and happy marriage.

In the late 1940s and early 1950s a team of young Protestant men traveled throughout the southeast with their campaigns to lead young people to Christ. Literally thousands of people were converted in the campaigns. Later, three of these young men continued into what is sometimes called "full-time Christian work." The fourth individual, a millionaire businessman from Texas, remains to this day an active lay preacher and churchman. The music leader of this four-man evangelistic team never married, but the other three men did marry. Two of these married men became ordained ministers and pastors of dynamic churches. Later the wives of each of the two ministers sought a divorce.

One of the ministers, Eric Daniels, had earlier suffered emotional problems. Overcome with grief and guilt because of his destructive behavior toward the woman he had loved and lost, the Reverend Daniels submitted his resignation to the church which he had served for many years. Although the church voted not to accept the resignation, he nevertheless carried through with it.

Dr. Aaron Livingston was for over twenty years the respected and beloved minister of a large church of a certain southeastern city. Both he and his congregation were shocked to learn that Mrs. Livingston, after thirty years of marriage, was going to Reno to file for divorce. Because Dr. Livingston had stood with his people through many of their personal crises, they were now ready to stand with him through his own terrible crisis. Well-known as a speaker and worker within his denomination, Dr. Livingston knew that he would not simply be thrown out in the cold, but the divorce was nonetheless a profound emotional blow to him.

Attractive Alice Beck, herself twice divorced but currently single, was a member of Dr. Livingston's church. After Mrs. Livingston's divorce became legal, Alice Beck wasted no time in manifesting her interest in Dr. Livingston, her pastor. A large number of the church members felt that Alice was not the woman whom their minister should be seeing, except as her pastor. Even more, they did not want her to take to herself eventually that official-unofficial title known as "The Minister's Wife." The church had apparently accepted the fact that Dr. Livingston was not the sort of personality who could live the rest of his years as a single adult. They expected that as he collected his wits and gradually worked through the excruciating ordeal of his divorce, he would eventually and in proper time marry someone who would make a good "minister's wife."

But as the romance between Dr. Livingston and Alice Beck began to develop, the church people began to pray for their minister and to express openly their fears that in marrying the twice-divorced Mrs. Beck he would be making a tragic mistake. However, the people failed to consider the power of the "romantic fever." Those who work professionally with teenagers know that a teenage courtship that is moving toward marriage cannot be opposed head-on. Such opposition usually helps to drive the youths together, as if the youths were combining forces and resources to counter the attack against them. The "romantic fever" is not limited to teenagers, and Dr. Livingston was certainly in the throes of it.

Like anxious parents, many of the church members longed for a dissolution of the romance between their beloved and respected pastor and Alice Beck. But they did not know how to make it happen. Neither wise as serpents nor harmless as doves in this situation, they were just people who were genuinely hurt, confused, eager to help, though unable to influence their minister's decision in the way they had hoped. One outsider recommended that the members find *other* charming, interesting, and eligible women to introduce to Dr. Livingston. But this recommendation was passed off as "unspiritual," and so Alice Beck became the second Mrs. Livingston. Having observed from a distance this awkward and painful ordeal, I am persuaded that had Dr. Livingston taken a wife more in keeping with the expectations of the relatively conservative congregation, he would today still be serving as the minister of this particular church. But whether Dr. Livingston could have loved a wife that met the church's requirements—that is another question.

Realizing that he and many of his dearest friends at the church had developed too many disagreements regarding his remarriage, Dr. Livingston began to let it be known that he was open to an invitation to become the minister of another church. It was not too long before representatives of another outstanding church called on him and eventually invited him to become the church's new minister. He accepted.

The Reverend Eric Daniels, however, is no longer in the ministry; instead, he is doing an entirely different type of work. He and Jean recently remarried—on their twenty-fifth wedding anniversary.

This year in a thriving town in Texas, Mr. Mark Mason, an active Unitarian, saw at a public meeting the wife of one of the town's Presbyterian ministers.

"Oh, I read in the paper that you will be moving to Mexico City soon," said Mark, desiring to wish the woman and her minister husband well in their new venture.

"No, that's my husband," she replied. "He will be taking a church there. The children and I will not be going with him."

Intending only to congratulate her because of her good fortune in going to Mexico City, the nonplussed Unitarian found himself instead in an awkward situation because it had not occured to him that a Presbyterian minister and his wife might end their marriage in divorce.

"Some things you just can't take for granted," Mark commented to a friend. Almost always a most tactful and thoughtful person, Mark simply was one of those persons who, like many of us, had not realized just how far divorce had reached into even the more traditional Christian churches.

A marriage and family counselor recently wrote, "Three clergymen and their wives parted company through divorce last year in my home town of Columbia, Missouri."[1] In Mark's town in Texas, a second Presbyterian minister and his wife had only recently parted company. In the city of Nashville, Tennessee, an effective and popular Southern Baptist evangelist and pastor is now raising cattle on his ranch. Having been divorced twice—once from the daughter of a prominent denominational leader—this former evangelist is no longer welcomed to the pulpits of the churches of his denomination. One fellow minister said of him, "I don't see how he can live with himself." Ironically, this fellow minister was himself at the time experiencing strains in his own marriage and even found it necessary to be away from his church for a number of weeks in order to receive psychotherapy. Strains in the marital relationship are nothing new, not even for ministers. John Wesley's wife was once observed dragging her noted husband around by the hair of his head. When Wesley's horse died, he wept and was visibly moved. When his wife died, he appeared less moved and disturbed.

The Apostle Paul wrote of the special gift of grace required for anyone who would live happily as a single adult. (See 1 Cor. 7:7.) Doubtless many wives of pastors and evangelists have felt that they, too, must have a special gift of grace to live happily in marriage. Indeed, there are times when practically every married couple has felt the need for an extra portion of grace to help them through what Paul calls "worldly cares."

The Churches and the Divorced

The hard fact is that divorce, even among many committed Christian leaders, has become a steady trend. Whether or not this trend can be turned back is still a matter of speculation. Even if divorce should remain at its present rate, the churches have the clear challenge to meet the fact of divorce in a Christian manner. Recently in the official Tennessee Baptist journal, one writer called on his fellow believers to find a more creative way of dealing with the divorced. On the one hand he wanted to protect the divorced from the overly solicitous, while on the other hand he wanted to insure that the divorced would not be excluded from the mainstream of the life of the churches. His stirring article set forth pointedly the dilemma which Christians now face. The title is: "Churches Must Minister to or Lose Divorced Persons."[2] Dr. David Edens saw clearly the need for Christians to develop practical and sensitive guidelines for relating to their divorced friends.[3]

Glamorizing Divorce

There is no point in denying that marriage has been glamorized and often over-advertised. It is not surprising, therefore, that a large number of couples have become disillusioned with marriage. At the same time, however, the trend toward *glamorizing divorce* needs to be called into question. A more realistic appraisal would seem to lead to the conclusion that the single life is best for some people, while marriage is best for others. Yet even this is too sweeping a generalization. Either marriage or the single life might be best *under certain conditions*. Furthermore, to speak of marriage *per se* may be to forget that Jane might be happily married to Kevin but unhappily married to Thomas. But suppose that Jane foolishly married Thomas rather than Kevin. Suppose that in her youth she failed to make use of her intelligence and allowed herself to enter a very poor life-long relationship. Looking back, we can see that marrying Thomas was a terrible mistake in the first place. But now that it has been made, should Jane simply seek a divorce from Thomas? Is that a live option for a Christian to take in rising above a costly blunder that was made in one's youth?

There is no point in obscuring the fact that both Christ and Paul clearly teach that divorce is a violation of the divine will. It has often been pointed out that because neither Christ nor Paul had ever been married, they could not fully understand the complex marriage relationship. But the Christian who possibly may be thinking of divorce, or that of a friend or relative, cannot take comfort in this thought, for the Christian is committed to the view that both Christ and Paul were inspired by God in their strict views on divorce. Still the question of divorce cannot simply be ignored by responsible Christians. If divorce is to be strictly proscribed, then what other alternatives are available for a married couple whose marriage has all the marks of either coming apart at the seams or becoming a meaningless and lifeless form?

Martin Luther and Prince Philipp

The great Protestant reformer Martin Luther received a letter from Philipp of Hesse, who had been forced into a political marriage at the age of nineteen. Looking back, we might wish to say that young Philipp had a choice even before he married. He should have refused to marry the young woman selected for him. But who can deny that social pressures, as well as other pressures, often influence us finite creatures to make less than perfectly rational decisions?[4]

Prince Philipp, writing to Luther, pointed out that he had come to be involved with a second woman, who, unlike Philipp's wife, was not frigid. Appealing to the Gospels, Luther insisted that divorce was impossible for even a Christian prince. That is, divorce could not be accepted as a Christian solution to the prince's desperate problem.

So, what was the solution that Luther offered? It was simple advice—the prince should bear his cross patiently and courageously. Unable, however, to find the grace to do this, Philipp finally asked Luther to help him to find a solution that he could actually live with as a finite human being. To this request, Luther, as Philipp's pastor, recommended that the Christian prince take the second woman as his second wife without abandoning his first wife. Divorce was strictly ruled out. But bigamy was, for Luther, a live Christian option for two reasons: (1) In the first place, he could find no clear scriptural injunction against it. (2) In the second place, the Bible records that various men of faith in the Bible had more than one wife at a time.[5] This may sound strange to the average suburban Christian today, but the Christian should not fall into the trap of thinking that options are dictated wholly from the local social setting in which one happened to grow up. Whatever we today may think of polygamy or bigamy, each Christian must ask, "What are the options that the sacred Scriptures themselves leave open to me?"

On another occasion, Pastor Luther was asked to consider the case of a Christian man whose wife's illness had simply eliminated all sexual intercourse between the couple. Presumably, no one was to blame for their tragic situation. She simply had ceased to function sexually because of certain malfunctions of her body. The Apostle Paul had long ago suggested that it was better to marry than to burn with sexual passion. (See 1 Corinthians 7:9.) But Luther was now confronted with a fellow believer who, despite being married, was still burning with unfulfilled sexual passion because he could not enjoy intercourse with his wife. Again, it was the Apostle Paul himself who had taught that not every Christian was able to completely control sexual passion as Paul himself had done. Such an achievement was, for Paul, a special gift of grace not bestowed on everyone, for "each man hath his own gift from God, one after this manner, and another after that." (1 Cor. 7:7 American Standard Version of 1901) Paul held that it was preferable for the single person to remain single, but he felt also that because of the sexual drive, many Christians would be well advised to marry rather than engage in sexual activity without being married. (See 1 Corinthians 7:8, 9.)

What, then, was Martin Luther to say to his fellow Christian who lacked Paul's special gift to live without experiencing strong sexual passion and whose tragic marital situation rendered impossible the normal sexual life of married persons? Was the man free to divorce his wife and marry a woman who could enjoy with him a happy sexual experience? Luther could not agree to divorce. So, once again, the Protestant pastor-reformer recommended that if the man simply could not live the rest of his married life without sexual intercourse, then he was free to take a second wife. Better to love and care for two wives than to forsake one's first wife for another woman.

A superficial look at Paul's words in 1 Corinthians might lead us to conclude that, for him, marriage was hardly more than a safety valve for sexual passion. Better to marry than to suffer unrelieved sexual passion! A more careful reading of Paul's other writings on marriage will reveal to us that marriage was, for him, much more than a pragmatic release of the sexual build-up. There is, in addition, the quality that we today call "loving companionship." Because of her illness, the wife of Luther's Christian friend may not have been able to engage in sexual intercourse, but that does not entail that she was a failure as a human female companion. Furthermore, with many others, I would go so far as to say that the marriage commitment binds us to stay with our spouse *especially* when she or he is ill—"in sickness and in health." Luther was too humane to recommend that the man simply abandon his wife in order to marry another.

If a Christian man or woman should come to me today with this same problem and ask for my considered advice, what should I say? What should you say? We might tell the person to pray for grace to abstain from all sexual intercourse until his or her permanently ill spouse should die. But we would have no right to specify how God would positively answer such a prayer. We are not in the business of second-guessing God's plans for each life. Nor are we in a position to proclaim that if the special gift of abstinence has not been granted, then the prayer of petition was not offered in sincerity or in faith.

I believe that Luther was more realistic and more Christian in his advice than some Christian writers today seem willing to concede. There is nothing especially Christian about sinking one's head in the sand, or hiding from hard facts that cause us pain or fail to square with our engrained expectations. If Christ enjoined Christians to be as harmless as doves, he enjoined them to be also as wise as serpents. But wisdom has little opportunity to grow in an atmosphere in which piety is confused with the failure to consider the hard realities of finite relationships, including marriage. The Christian doctrine of human finitude and imperfection should serve to hold in check some of our illusions about what behavior to expect from even Christian leaders.

This is another way of saying that perfect solutions to problems of human relationships, whether within or without marriage, are not something that Christians can demand. We may all covet a neat and tidy world on earth, where human interactions will always work smoothly, at least among committed Christians; but a careful reading of the Bible shows that even the best of Christians do not always resolve in a desirable way their differences of opinion and temperament.

Marriage and Worldly Troubles

In advising the church at Corinth, Paul warns that if the unmarried do marry, they will have "worldly troubles" and will not be "free from anxieties." (1 Cor. 7:28,32 R.S.V.) He seemed not to live under the illusions that some modern Christians do when they recommend marriage as the ideal life for almost everyone. Paul, by contrast, says plainly that "he who refrains from marriage will do better." (1 Cor. 7:38 R.S.V.) Earlier he had expressed his wish "that all were as myself," namely single and without sexual frustration (1 Cor. 7:7).

The Relationship Between Paul and Barnabas

Paul regarded himself as quite special in being able to control his sexual passion, perhaps to the point where sexual arousal was not even a part of his life-style. But in getting along with an intimate and close companion in such a way as to avoid serious disagreement and even rifts in the relationship, Paul was far from completely successful. For example, the companionship between Paul and Barnabas was profound and meaningful, but ultimately it ended in what may be described as a tragic divorce. A careful look at this Christian companionship should be instructive to those Christians wishing to have a deeper understanding of what is and is not possible for Christians who live both in the world and under grace.

Paul admonished all married couples to live up to the sexual agreements implicit in their marital bond, (see 1 Corinthians 7:3) just as he admonished church members not to divide themselves into factions (see 1 Corinthians 1:10-15).

But despite the fact that he and Barnabas had worked together faithfully as fellow missionaries, apparently for a number of years, the two of them reached a point where their conflicts could no longer be resolved. When Barnabas wanted to take John Mark with them on their return visit to the churches in every city in which they had previously preached, Paul would not hear of it. Mark had left them once before, and Paul was not disposed to give him another chance. The rift between Paul and Barnabas became so serious that they could no longer be reconciled to the task of working as companions one with the other. Splitting up their missionary alliance, they went their separate ways—Barnabas with John Mark, and Paul with a new partner named Silas.

The Reaction of the Churches

We can only guess at how the churches reacted upon hearing of the falling out and separation of Paul and Barnabas. We can easily imagine a letter being sent to Paul from Philemon, whom Paul had earlier advised to be reconciled to Onesimus, a fellow Christian with whom Philemon had experienced a falling out. Perhaps a husband and wife approached Paul to remind him that, after all, it was he who had once helped them to avoid divorce; and now they were willing to help him to avoid the dissolution of the beautiful alliance between Paul and Barnabas. Indeed, we cannot help but wonder what influence for reconciliation the churches sought to bring to bear on these two noted missionaries. Some of the churches may have sent delegates saying in effect the following:

> Our beloved Paul and Barnabas, your brotherly love and work together as co-laborers in Christ have become a holy example before the world. Do not now stain your public witness for Christ by continuing with the divorce between yourselves. What will the world think of the preaching of harmony in Christ and brotherly love if you—our beloved Paul and Barnabas—cannot overcome your strife one with the other? We, therefore, respectfully beseech you to take your division to Christ in prayer, to present your conflict before the altar of the Father, and to invite the Holy Spirit of God to bring you peace in the place of dissension.

Kenneth and Deloras

Kenneth and Deloras, married for eighteen years and members of the large Protestant Church not too far from their home, have raised two fine boys to their teenage years. The parents own a camping trailer, visit now and then with the boys' grandparents, and have a beautiful new house in a pleasant area of town. Things appeared to be going well between Kenneth and Deloras until one day Kenneth dropped an emotional bomb. He informed Deloras that without delay he was moving out—leaving her! Later, their minister, coming to visit as an ambassador of reconciliation, eventually was forced to realize that the separation was deep and profound. Just as the friends of Barnabas and Paul might have felt frustrated when they finally realized that the separation between the two missionaries was final, so the minister felt frustrated in his unsuccessful attempt to prevent the rift between Kenneth and Deloras from developing beyond reconcilation. But there are different ministries of reconciliation and healing. After divorce, there are still two people who need support, guidance, and the hand of Christian fellowship.

A Variety of Separations and Divorce Among Christians

The phenomenon of separation and divorce between Christian husband and wife, between Christians friends, or between groups of Christians has never been looked at realistically by a number of Christians. And understandably so. After preaching and teaching that Christ is the real hope of harmony in the world, Christians are quite naturally pained at the thought that not even Christians can always live together in harmony. However, in this modern day, when divorce between husband and wife has become epidemic, the churches need to take a good look at themselves. In the first place, those of us who are in the churches have split off from one another for all manner of causes and reasons. Secondly, we have often separated in anger and bitter denunciation of one another. Thirdly, we have taken each other to court or have in various ways used political and legal power to gain some advantage over one another. It is with shame that we recall the way that orthodox Christians pushed their fellow believer, Roger Williams, out of their midst because of his views on religious toleration and liberty.

What I am suggesting here is that the churches ought to understand divorce much better than they do because over the centuries they have manifested toward one another all the hurtful and tragic marks of married couples going through the shattering and bitter experience of divorce. Evangelical Christians in particular, in their genuine concern to uphold the ideal of life-long marriage, have sometimes cast stones at the divorced when they themselves have not always been able to control bitter strife, dissension, separation, and divorce among and within the churches.

We may be thankful that the divorce between husband and wife has generally not experienced the *violent* animosity that at different times in history various churches have expressed toward one another. To be sure, as with divorce between husband and wife, so with divorce between Christians there is the tendency of each party to see itself as the innocent victim and the other as the basic cause of the rift. Through centuries of trial and error, as well as grace and forgiveness, the churches have learned to live better with their own ecclesiastical separations and divorces. Sometimes even attempts to "remarry" have proved successful between churches or denominations, while at other times a "friendly divorce" has come about, or at least has developed many years after the initial disruption and separation.

Despite Christ's prayer that his followers "may all be one," and despite the biblical injunction that husband and wife together become one, the truth is that degrees and varieties of separations and divorces remain a cold fact of even the Christian life. Therefore, it would seem to be the course of wisdom and Christian responsibility to rethink afresh the entire question of at least marriage and divorce. Beyond a certain point, it would have been harmful had the early New Testament churches exerted pressure on Paul and Barnabas to heal their division. The churches apparently learned to live with this tragic break-up and continued to do what they could to foster the kingdom of Christ. Fortunately, the two missionaries continued to be welcome at the churches and were allowed to carry on their ministry without suffering the scorn and reproach of their fellow believers. Similarly, the bewildering fact is that Christian marriages sometimes grow stale or develop irreversibly harmful patterns that lead to either a meaningless marriage or a divorce. Churches need not glorify divorce in the way that some sensationalists do, but they *do* need to face more realistically and compassionately their responsibility to the separated and divorced among them.

Fortunately, the resources of Christian friends and church members can sometimes be utilized to help restore a precarious marriage to a point of acceptable stability and mutual reward. By rethinking more profoundly the marriage relationship and its real and serious problems, the evangelical Christian churches may become more responsible in helping their members to live up to the marital ideal. These Christians regard marriage as a divine institution ordained of God, but this in no way entails that common sense and accumulated practical knowledge, as well as sociological and psychological research, cannot all be utilized for the benefit of so worthy an institution as marriage. And when a marriage finally fails, the evangelical Christian cannot with consistency react as if the divorced person is an object of taboo and absolute defilement. Such may be the response of certain pagan and primitive religions, but it cannot be the response and attitude of Christians who believe in the working of divine grace.

The Case of Adultery

One of the first things that Christians perhaps need to reexamine long and hard is the deep-seated assumption that adultery is a sufficient ground for divorce. Many people take it as a fact that adultery ought necessarily to lead to divorce and that whoever divorces a spouse because of his or her adultery is making the right choice, a choice which God not only accepts but requires.

The book of Hosea makes it quite clear that adultery need not lead to divorce. This is certainly not to say that overt adultery is given the perfect stamp of approval. Far from it. Nevertheless, the book of Hosea richly embodies the teaching of Christ that the believer must be prepared to forgive and accept seventy times seven—even in the case of adultery. I acknowledge that this may sound strange and even radical to some Christians, but I am attempting to draw out the implications of the teachings of Scripture rather than reflect what has been loosely characterized as middle-class morality.

The truth is that in every marriage certain practices by one spouse are accepted by the other spouse even though the latter may not approve of them. Does this mean, then, that adultery is something that a person, while strongly disapproving of it in his or her spouse, can nevertheless live with? Surely this cannot be! Or can it? Let us turn to the Bible for insight into this question.

The Bible on Adultery

There can be no serious doubt that the Bible throughout does condemn adultery as not a part of the ideal form of marriage. The Bible also condemns lying. In the Ten Commandments both adultery and lying are proscribed. We may suppose, nevertheless, that there are some Christian marriages in which at least some lying of some degree has taken place, perhaps one lie a week or a month, sometimes a serious lie of terrible consequences, and sometimes a lie of apparently less harmful consequences.

Now the critical question is this: Can evangelical Christians say that lying is in God's eyes a legitimate ground for divorce? Traditionally they have said that only adultery offers such a ground. Buy why? Presumably, Jesus designated adultery to be the *only* acceptable grounds for divorce. I will quote the noted passage from the Gospel of Matthew:

> *But I say to you that everyone who divorces his wife, except on the ground of* unchastity, *makes her an adulteress; and whoever marries a divorced woman commits adultery.* (*Matt. 5:32 R.S.V., emphasis added*)

The New English Bible agrees with the Revised Standard Version on using the word *unchastity,* whereas the Goodspeed translation and the Williams translation agree on using the word *unfaithfulness.* Both the King James Version and the American Standard Version of 1901 use the word *fornication.*

There is honest debate among Christians as to what exactly Jesus had in mind to specify as the only ground for divorce, a ground that would not render the divorce itself as an act of adultery. It is significant that *neither* the Gospel of Mark *nor* the Gospel of Luke includes the clause that reads: "except on the ground of unchastity." The clause occurs *only* in the Gospel of Matthew. When all the Gospels were first written, each was presented to local congregations of Christians, which meant that many decades may have passed before all the Gospels were collected together in one place or in most of the churches. If that is the case, then all those Christians who did not have access to the Gospel of Matthew were reading, at best, other Gospels that provide *absolutely no ground for divorce.*

Neither Luke nor Mark records Jesus as permitting any legitimate ground for divorce in God's sight. According to these two Gospels, whoever divorces and remarries commits adultery. Period. No conditionals, no exceptions. Paul in a letter to the Corinthian Christians tells them not even to seek divorce even if they are married to unbelievers. He does concede that if the unbelieving member of the marriage refuses to live with his or her Christian spouse, then divorce is permitted in order to maintain peace. "For God has called us to peace." (See 1 Corinthians 7:12-16.)

But there is some disagreement as to whether Paul leaves open the option of *remarriage* for the Christian who has been compelled to divorce his or her unbelieving spouse. Paul says that in such a case the Christian is "not bound," but it remains unclear as to what exactly the apostle had in mind to say. (See 1 Corinthians 7:15.) I personally think that he is saying no more than that a Christian is "not bound" in marriage to an unbeliever who refuses to live with his or her Christian partner. Paul is not leaving open the option of remarriage. But I acknowledge that this passage is insufficiently clear for me to insist on this interpretation.

Christ's Ideal of Marriage

Some New Testament scholars conclude that *the original copy of the Gospel of Matthew contained no clause at all allowing divorce on the ground of unchastity.*[6] These scholars support their conclusion primarily in two ways. First, appealing to the overall teachings of Jesus, they contend that this special clause does not fit with the general tone of his non-legalistic ethic. Second, they remind us that, while reporting Christ's words on divorce and adultery, neither the Gospel of Mark nor the Gospel of Luke contains this clause in question. The omission is regarded as quite significant. This conclusion need not, however, be interpreted as standing in conflict with the belief that the Bible is the inerrant revelation of God. It merely conjectures, with some reason, that the clause "except on the ground of unchastity" was not a part of the Gospel of Matthew *to begin with*. The clause was added *later*, perhaps as a scribal comment in the margin, a comment which still later was inserted into the main body by a copyist who erroneously thought that the comment had simply been both left out by mistake and added on to the margin when the mistake was discovered. There is some reason to accept this conjecture, but I cannot in my own mind decide whether there is *sufficient* reason to do so. In any case, even if Christ does *permit* divorce on the ground of unchastity, we still have to determine whether he *requires* divorce on such a ground.

What Is Unchastity?

But what is unchastity? Or, to use the Goodspeed and Williams translations, what is marital *unfaithfulness?* Some Christians regard it as sexual intercourse between a married person and someone who is not his or her spouse. According to this view, if Kenneth is now, or has been, sexually involved with another woman, then Deloras has legitimate cause in God's eyes to divorce Kenneth without herself being judged by God as an adulteress.

But, still, it does seem strange that neither the Gospel of Mark nor the Gospel of Luke mentions this legitimate cause. Basil Atkinson, a New Testament scholar, is led to write, "In contrast to Moses, our Lord forbids divorce absolutely,"[7] Atkinson claims that what Jesus is referring to as a ground of divorce is sexual intercourse *before*, not after, the marriage ceremony. According to this interpretation, Jesus was referring to "unfaithfulness on the part of a woman *before* marriage. If this [unfaithfulness] is discovered subsequent to marriage, the Lord's words oblige the husband to put the woman away because in God's sight *there has been no marriage.* "[8] Akinson contends that according to Scripture, "every woman belongs by nature in God's sight to *the first man with whom she has sexual intercourse, and to 'marry' her during the lifetime of that man is to commit adultery."* [9] It follows, on this view, that it would be immoral for a man to divorce his legitimate wife. Why? Because such would imply something about his wife that is untrue. It would imply that he had recently discovered that her *first* experience of sexual intercourse had been with another man. By divorcing her, he would in effect be nullifying the marriage ceremony on the ground that she came to the marriage under the false pretense of being a virgin. If in fact she had been a virgin up to the time of the marriage, then to attempt to "put her away" would be to malign her character by falsely accusing her.

Needless to say, Atkinson's interpretation raises some serious questions. For example, imagine a man who has lived with his wife—or what he had thought was his wife—for four decades. Then he discovers that when she was seventeen and unmarried she had sexual intercourse with another man. If Atkinson's interpretation is correct, then the man she has been living with for forty years *cannot* any longer live with this woman. Why? Because she is in fact another man's wife. Indeed, according to this view, she has been living in adultery for forty years!

Well, suppose the deceived man "puts the woman away." What is she to do after that? If Henry, with whom she first had sexual intercourse over forty years ago, is still alive, can she in the eyes of God marry him? Indeed *must* she marry him? On the other hand, if Henry is himself now "married" to another woman, Gale, should he first put Gale away in order to begin a marital relationship with the woman with whom he had sexual intercourse over forty years ago?

According to Atkinson's interpretation, the Old Testament simply gave the male more sexual liberties than it gave the female. Presumably a woman was not even *permitted* by God to put her husband away if she discovered that he had experienced sexual intercourse before marriage. This would seem to be a morality of double standards, at least on this one point. It even makes sexual intercourse appear to be something of a brand that the man puts on a woman, but not a brand that the woman can put on a man.

I must admit that after studying carefully the teachings of Christ on divorce, and after studying various commentaries on the Gospels, I cannot find one interpretation to be more compelling than some of the strong rival interpretations. I will not here go into all the viable interpretations. It is significant that in Atkinson's view, if premarital sexual intercourse happened between two young people, then they are in God's eyes married and are, therefore, living in adultery if they continue to live with anyone other than that person with whom they had their first experience of sexual intercourse.

Many Christians will agree that premarital sexual intercourse is to be avoided. But sincere disagreement arises when an impulsive sexual act by two youths is declared by Atkinson and others to be the actual entrance into a marriage relationship. Marriage is far more than sexual intercourse, and to enter it voluntarily or involuntarily on sexual grounds alone is to turn one youthful wayward act into a pathetic and tragic marriage of many years (assuming it will not eventually end in divorce).

Some Harmful Consequences of Divorce

According to the nineteenth chapter of Matthew, the disciples of Jesus, after hearing his strong views on divorce, remarked that to marry did not seem to be the expedient or practical thing to do. Jesus acknowledged that not everyone could live by his stiff precept on marriage and divorce. (See Matthew 19:10-11.) Standing in opposition to many centuries of a male-dominated tradition on marriage and divorce, Jesus presented the revolutionary teaching that adultery was not something that only women could be guilty of. Men, too, are bound by the marriage commitment. As one New Testament scholar puts it, "In marriage there are equal obligations before God."[10]

It is safe to say that the ideal marriage as Jesus and Paul portrayed it is that of a life-long union between man and woman. In my judgment, the Christ of the Gospels does not provide any legitimate ground at all for divorce. On the other hand, by admitting that not everyone can live up to the highest ideal, he *may* be suggesting that divorce is a kind of concession to the weakness of the human make-up.

In light of the above two paragraphs, I wish to propose in the following chapters an alternative to divorce and remarriage for married couples who, while unable to live up to the highest ideal of marriage, nevertheless still have a profound and mutually respectful companionship. But before explicating this proposal, I will make a relevant comment on divorce.

In many cases (but not all) divorce is a devastating experience playing havoc with the lives of the children. Furthermore, if the divorced parent who takes the children does eventually marry another person, then the children often have a very difficult time of adjusting to the second marriage. The problems involved may prove to be overwhelming to the children.

V

MARRIAGE
AND THE WEAKNESS
OF THE FLESH

Admitting Marital Strife and Conflict of Interests

Married couples who are committed believers in Christ cannot help feeling uncomfortable when they read or hear the following words of Christ: "Be ye therefore perfect, even as your Father which is in heaven is perfect." (Matt. 5:48 K.J.V.) If any human being knows of some of our weaknesses and imperfections, it is our marriage partner. We may be able to restrain our anger pretty well outside the house, but our spouse knows that we are a million miles from being in perfect control of all our anger and passion. Later I will return to Christ's statement on perfection. I wish now to quote words by the Apostle Paul, words that deserve to be read and reread by Christians who sometimes think that they have reached a state of perfect love. Speaking of himself, Paul penned the following moving passage:

> For I delight in the law of God after the inward man: But I see another law in my members, warring against the law of my mind, and bringing me into captivity to the law of sin which is in my members... So then with the mind I myself serve the law of God; but with the flesh the law of sin. (Rom. 7:22-23, 25 K.J.V.)

The point here is that even within *himself* the sincere Christian believer must undergo a certain amount of strife and conflict. It should not surprise us, therefore, to learn of strife and conflict within a marriage, even a Christian marriage. Paul indicated that he struggled regularly with himself, and many husbands and wives will acknowledge that marriage itself contains periods of difficult struggle and strife between them. But, still, some couples seem to feel that it is not quite right to admit even to themselves that they are sometimes in conflict with one another. Paul thought it wise to acknowledge honestly the personal conflict within himself, and we could add that a reasonably mature Christian marriage will honestly acknowledge a measure of strife and struggle within the marriage.

Esther and Al Carter had been married for only a short while when they had a very heated dispute with one another. The next day Al was very upset, for he had always believed that true Christians did not relate to each other in such a way. He began to doubt whether he was a genuinely spiritual person. He even had a passing thought that just maybe he had married the wrong person. The thought frightened him. Had he married contrary to God's purpose? Before the wedding, he and Esther had prayed often about their marriage. But had they really listened to God's answer? The burden of thinking that he had married the wrong woman—a woman whom God had perhaps selected for *another man*—was sometimes almost more than Al Carter could bear. He simply had not expected either to feel this way or to have had the heated squabble with his wife.

Al might have been spared a lot of unnecessary agony had he studied more carefully the letters of the Apostle Paul. From Paul's first letter to the Corinthians, Al would have learned that to be married is to be in conflict sometimes. As a ministerial student and pastor of a small church, Al's free time was very limited. It bothered him that he seemed never to have time to be alone with Esther. In his first letter to the Corinthians, Paul offered the following very sound insight into the phenomenon of divided loyalty in a Christian marriage:

I want you to be free from anxieties. The unmarried man is anxious about the affairs of the Lord, how to please the Lord; but the married man is anxious about worldly affairs, how to please his wife, and his interests are divided. And the unmarried woman or girl is anxious about the affairs of the Lord, how to be holy in body and spirit; but the married woman is anxious about worldly affairs, how to please her husband. (1 Cor. 7:32-34 R.S.V., emphasis added)

While recommending that Christians remain single so that they would spend less time and attention on "worldly affairs," Paul also made it clear that to marry is no sin (1 Cor. 7:28). This means that to have Al's kind of divided interests is itself no sin. It is simply a lot of trouble sometimes. Of course, when a person's interests are divided between his spouse and the Lord, then it should come as no surprise that attention to some of the details of service to the Lord will have to be cut back. To state this in very practical terms, some religious activities may have to be given up or reduced in order that one's relationship with one's spouse can be nurtured and cared for. Sometimes Al failed to remember that the commitment of marriage bound him to attend to his wife's needs (and she to his needs), even if it meant placing to the side certain special religious practices and works.

When husband and wife sometimes dispute over whether to attend an enjoyable dinner engagement or to attend a Bible conference (or something similar), they must not suppose that one of these options is right while the other is wrong. Rather, it may be nothing more than a case of *two good* opportunities, only one of which they can take advantage of together. Conflicts like this particular one should not give rise to guilt or accusation but to practical negotiations. Al would not—or should not—feel guilty if he desires both to go out with his wife for a delightful social evening and to be involved with the Bible conference. The feeling of ambivalence or uncertainty as to what choice to make is an experience of human *finitude*, which should not be confused with *guilt*. The human necessity of having to reject one good option in favor of another is not something in itself that should create guilt responses.

To be sure, there is the sort of person who seems to prefer to go through life without having to *choose* between two or more good options. For some reason, when he selects one good option over another good one, he feels disloyal or guilty. Instead of being glad that he had many good options and was able to select and enjoy one of them, he becomes preoccupied with the rejected options. They haunt him sorely, as if they were ghosts following him.

Such a person has mastered the technique of guaranteeing that he will be miserable regardless of the circumstances. In a very humorous book Dan Greenburg tells how a mother can work it so that in a good situation her son will always end up feeling very bad:

> (1) Give your son Marvin two sportshirts as a present. The first time he wears one of them, look at him sadly and say in your Basic Tone of Voice: "The other one you didn't like?"[1]

This is the perfect "double bind."

Unfortunately, some people confuse this feeling of the double bind with being exceedingly spiritual. They think that feeling guilty most of the time will somehow prove that they are serious Christians. In reality, they reveal themselves to be somber people who have somehow missed the theme of joy that vibrates in practically every page that Paul wrote.

We have all met Christians who seem to want to give back to God their freedom of choice. Apparently believing that doing God's will is a kind of passive submission, they dislike choosing and even pray that God will deprive them of options to choose from.

Very often when people fall into this gloomy way of life, it is because they either have been taught that such is expected of the true Christian or have been rewarded by others for practicing this way of life. They are rewarded by being praised, shown special consideration, or given other social acknowledgments. In Bible conferences or other Christian study groups, some of these people may come to see that their gloomy way of life is not required Christian behavior. Upon seeing this, they may still be unable to change their old ways without additional help from fellow Christians. By associating with the more healthy-minded evangelical Christians, the gloomy ones may observe that it is possible to live a life of Christian enjoyment on earth in the face of conflicts and divided interests. Also fellow Christians can encourage, inspire, and motivate their new friends by reinforcing active decision-making and by paying little regard to the old habit of using guilt and passiveness as a badge of righteousness.

Jealousy, Envy, and Anger in the Christian Marriage

It is of practical importance to ask why it is that some Christian couples resist admitting that sometimes they experience strife, anger, resentment, envy, and jealousy. The answer is quite simple: these negative traits are condemned strongly in the Bible. The Apostle Paul wrote:

> Now the works of the flesh are plain; immorality, impurity, licentiousness, idolatry, sorcery, enmity strife, jealousy, anger, selfishness, dissension, party spirit, envy, drunkenness, carousing, and the like. I warn you, as I warned you before, that those who do such things shall not inherit the kingdom of God. (*Gal. 5:19-21 R.S.V., emphasis added*)

Now those are pretty strong words! In the quotation above, I have placed in italics those particular words which are more likely to describe even the Christian marriage under certain conditions and at various times. Let us look carefully at what Paul said in this passage. In effect, he placed anger in the same category as idolatry and carousing. It is no wonder, therefore, that Christians are reluctant to admit having periods of anger (as well as envy, jealousy, strife, and selfishness) in their own lives. But not to admit strife and the like is to commit still another sin, namely, the sin of lying. "If we say that we have no sin, we deceive ourselves, and the truth is not in us . . . . If we say that we have not sinned, we make him a liar, and his word is not in us." (1 John 1:8,10 K.J.V.)

The Christian seems to be caught between what Martin

Luther called the devil and the deep blue sea. On the one hand, he knows full well that he sins daily. Indeed, it is because he is a Christian that he is more sensitive than some people to certain sins. And yet on the other hand, he must consider also the following passage: "He that committeth sin is of the devil . . . . Whosoever is born of God doth not commit sin." (1 John 3:8-9 K.J.V.) This *seems* to imply that if a Christian husband gets angry with his wife, or if his wife shows any jealousy regarding him, then the two of them are of the devil and not of God. Indeed, the Scripture says, "Whosoever is born of God doth not commit sin; for his [i.e., God's] seed remaineth in him: and *he cannot sin,* because he is born of God." (1 John 3:9, italics added)

If these passages are not discouraging enough, there is yet another: "For whatsoever is born of God overcometh the world . . . . " (1 John 5:4 K.J.V.) But the sincere Christian sometimes feels that he is not always victorious in overcoming the world. Sometimes the world beats him back. Often he senses his weaknesses and imperfections. For example, today David is feeling guilty because last night he spoke very sharply to his wife Evelyn and said some unkind things to her. She in turn continued the strife and anger by her own manifestation of selfishness. Indeed, every Christian married person knows sometimes that he or she ought to apologize and even change some habits and ways in order to pave the way for a better marriage. And sometimes a person does improve. But there remains still so much more that ought to be done that simply is not done. To realize this is one thing. But it is another—and something that is even more painful to the Christian—to have to read the following words of Scripture: "Whoever knows what is right to do and fails to do it, for him it is sin." (James 4:17 R.S.V.) Another translation reads as follows: "Therefore to him that knoweth to do good, and doeth *it* not, to him it is sin." (James 4:17 K.J.V.)

Again, it is not surprising that Christian married couples sometimes pretend that they have no strife or envy in their relationship or pretend that they always live up fully to the highest

ideal of marriage. But this pretense creates its own problems—
self-deception, guilt feelings, and even disguised hostility toward
one's spouse.

But What Is a Christian Supposed to Do?

One of the great tragedies of many Christians is that they
have a poor understanding of the biblical view of what it means
to live a Christian life. By not seeing the Bible in its wholeness,
they absorb distorted interpretations that sometimes have very
destructive consequences in their everyday lives. Consequently,
trying to follow Christ seems to become, for them, something
oppressive and wearisome. They live more out of guilt and fear
than out of Christian realism, grace, and joy. It is unfortunate
that so many Christian couples seem to be such dreary souls.

But what else could be expected of these sincere but unfortunate Christians? On the one hand, they believe that Scripture
commands them to be perfect. On the other hand, they know
down deep that they do sin and are terribly imperfect. Furthermore, they have nagging doubts about whether there is any way
to attain perfection on earth. What is a Christian supposed to do
upon reading that whoever commits sin is of the devil? It is not
surprising that sometimes one even doubts that he or she was ever
a genuine Christian believer in the first place. If being born of
God means overcoming the world, then *no* Christian believer
seems really to overcome the world *if* to overcome the world
means never falling prey to envy, strife, anger, jealousy, selfishness, and the like.

Getting Things in Biblical Perspective

However, this whole question of the believer's sin must be
placed in New Testament perspective. It is true that Christ of the
Gospels demanded perfection. It is true also that the author of
the First Epistle of John said that "whatsoever is born of God
overcometh the world . . . . " But if we read very carefully the
rest of what this latter passage had to say, we will gain a profoundly new picture of the New Testament view of human sin. I

will quote the entire verse: "For whatsoever is born of God over-cometh the world: and *this* is the victory that overcometh the world, even our *faith.*" (1 John 5:4 K.J.V., italics added) The plain teaching here is that it is the believer's faith in Christ, and not the believer's works that opens the door to the victory over the world. The New English Bible gives an even better transla-tion of the meaning: "The victory that defeats the world is our faith . . . . "

In the Greek in which the New Testament was written, the word that is often translated *faith* might also be translated *trust*. Especially in his Letter to the Romans and his Letter to the Galatians, Paul emphasized over and over that the believer's righteousness is in reality nothing that *he* produces, but rather is the righteousness of Christ. Christ's righteousness, then, is *given freely* to the believer, who simply *trusts* in God's grace to forgive and accept him even though *in himself* the believer continues to sin! As Paul said, "For we hold that a man is justified by faith [i.e., trust in God's grace] *apart from works of law.*"(Rom. 3:28 R.S.V., italics added) Paul made it clear that it was not the good works of Abraham that rendered Abraham righteous, but the grace of God which the patriarch received by faith or trust. (See Romans 4:1-5.)

Marriage and Christian Realism

What conclusions regarding Christian marital relationships can be drawn from the above discussion of divine grace and human trust? The first conclusion is that Christians do engage everyday in anger, strife, envy, and other sins. On earth these sins are not likely to cease altogether among Christians. If your marriage has strife and anger in it, this does not mean that you are not a faithful and true Christian. For, according to New Testament teaching, your victory over sin is a matter of *God's work of grace in Christ*, not of your own work. The truth is that you will continue to sin against your marriage partner, but this sin will not be counted against you as a believer inasmuch as God's grace in Christ is victorious over it. To receive Christ by faith or trust is to receive his victory over sin.

Of course, this does not mean that you are free to cease trying to control strife, envy, and the like in your marriage. But it does mean that if you and your wife are not always successful in your interpersonal relationships, you should not brood over it or think that your marriage is a complete failure. Furthermore, by seeing your marriage in the perspective of Christian realism, you can give yourself some elbow room for *enjoying* your marriage despite its strife, anger, and the like. Indeed, *a marriage can be ruined because too much is expected from it.* It simply is not biblical to suppose that the Christian ideal of marriage is the highest. There are many ideals of marriage that are higher than the Christian, and that is perhaps one reason why those ideals sometimes do a lot of harm. The Christian ideal of marriage is always tempered with a heavy dose of Christian realism regarding the propensity of human beings to come into conflict with one another and to do harm to one another.

To speak plainly, you cannot realistically expect your spouse to change completely all of his bad practices and attitudes. If you divorce and marry someone else, that person will also prove to be in strife and conflict with you on some matters of great importance. I remember hearing of a minister who asked all those in the congregation who had never had conflict with his or her marriage partner to raise their hands. While the hands were still raised, the minister then said to the rest of the congregation,

> I want you to look around to see who has his or her hand raised, for it is to these people that I wish to address my sermon today. My text for the sermon is, ''Thou shalt not bear false witness.''

Christians are not being hypocritical if, while representing themselves as ambassadors of Christ, they know secretly that their own marriages are not perfectly harmonious. There simply are no perfectly harmonious marriages, and to pretend that one has such a perfect marriage would be hyprocitical. The witness that a Christian gives to the world is not to superior righteousness, but to the grace of God and to God's willingness to use frail and imperfect human beings to carry forth his ministry of reconciliation.

If Your Spouse Becomes Obese

One of America's greatest evangelists was D.L. Moody, who led perhaps a million people to faith in Christ. Yet Moody was undeniably a glutton with a big bay window. Dr. Billy Graham once stated frankly that Moody was guilty of the sin of gluttony and that Moody ate himself to an early grave. Almost every day Moody committed this sin. The Bible strongly condemns it as a very wicked practice. (See Proverbs 23:20.) In fact, it was one of those sins that the book of Deuteronomy counted as rebellion, which could lead to one's being stoned to death. (See Deuteronomy 21:20; Proverbs 28:7.)

Knowing full well what the Apostle Paul said about the human body serving as the temple of God's Spirit, Moody was never able to give up his practice of eating excessively and immoderately. I will quote here Paul's stern words against those who would thoughtlessly or willfully impair their own health:

> Do you not know that you are God's temple and that God's Spirit dwells in you? If any one destroys God's temple, God will destroy him. For God's temple is holy, and that temple you are. (1 Cor. 3:16 R.S.V.)

According to Billy Graham, "Gluttony is the epitome of human selfishness." And if that is not plain enough, Dr. Graham has added, "It is a sin because it is a physical expression of the philosophy of *materialism*."[2] Doubtless Graham was correct when he stated frankly that gluttony is "a sin that most of us commit, but few of us ever mention."[3] Probably one reason that there are so few sermons on gluttony today is that too many ministers and church leaders are practicing it daily.

Yet the truth seems to be that this particular sin is creating a kind of divorce in marriages in the sense that it literally kills and therefore separates a number of husbands and wives from each other every month. Gluttony or excessive eating contributes to high blood pressure and other reactions that increase the percentages of heart disease as well as certain other diseases. During the Second World War, Mr. and Mrs. Fred Ponder experienced a serious crisis in their marriage when Fred became romantically involved with another woman. But eventually the involvement was dissolved, and today the Ponders are an elderly Christian couple working faithfully in their church. If Fred, who is very moderate in his eating habits, had been a glutton, his wife might very well be a widow today. In terms of severity of consequences, extreme gluttony in some cases has more disruptive and permanent harmful effects on marriage than does adultery.

Yet, D. L. Moody's wife did not even think of filing for divorce because of her husband's immoderate eating practice, which led to his early death. However, one day, while talking to a group of people about what they expected from their marriage partners, I was surprised to learn that they expected their partners not to become inordinately fat. They indicated that to gain excessive weight because of immoderate eating habits is in some sense to break faith with one's spouse. I suspect that when most of us in our imagination picture Christ, Paul, and Peter, we think of them as at least moderate in their weight, certainly not fat. Today, however, a number of Christians have become obese or inordinately heavy.

In talking further to people about how they felt about their spouse putting on a big bay window or developing large hunks of "flab," I learned that many of them felt that the "guilty" partner was at best very thoughtless and inconsiderate in putting on "flab." Probing further, I learned that if one partner takes care of his appearance and tries not to look obese, then he may feel betrayed when his spouse seems not to care about her own appearance. People sometimes seem to identify physically with their spouses, so much so that when one partner looks "flabby," it is taken as a bad reflection on the other. Sometimes a certain resentment builds up because an inordinately fat person seems to be saying the following to his or her spouse: "I do not care that I am a bad reflection on you."

Often this whole phenomenon of gluttony and obesity reveals a lot about some serious conflicts between husband and wife, although it would be a mistake to think that this is true in

every case. Marriage counselors report that excessive eating sometimes contributes to marital conflict and sometimes is a by-product
of unresolved marital conflict.

It is not my intention here to say that every Christian
should embark on a strict diet if he is obese. Those people who
do not eat very much seldom understand the powerful "psychological need" for food that some people develop. In some situations.
Christian couples simply have to learn to live with the obesity
of one of them, just as Mrs. Moody learned to live with her
husband's obesity. In other situations, practical steps are possible
for overcoming gluttony.

The noted psychoanalyst, Dr. Robert Lindner, told of the
uncontrollable hunger of Laura, a young woman who came to
him for help. He wrote:

> Laura had two faces. The one I saw that morning was
> hideous. Swollen like a balloon at the point of bursting,
> it was a caricature of a face, the eyes lost in pockets
> of swollen flesh and shining feverishly with a sick glow,
> the nose buried between bulging cheeks spattered with
> blemishes, the chin an oily shadow of mocking human
> contour; and somewhere in the mass of fat a crazy-angled
> carmined hole was her mouth.[4]

Jesus was moved with compassion when he saw lepers, but some
people are moved more by revulsion than compassion when they
see obesity that is taken to the degree exemplified by Laura. I am
happy to report that in time and with much work, Dr. Lindner
was able to cure Laura's obesity.

Unfortunately, this is not always the case with everyone.
What I wish to say, therefore, is that not every marriage has to
be alike regarding excessive eating and obesity. Some sincere
Christian couples simply cannot overcome the obesity of at least
one of them. But they nevertheless learn to live with it and to
love each other all the same. Mrs. Moody dearly loved her husband until his dying day.

Indeed, it deserves note that, in so far as I know, no
church or organization of Christian ministers ever turned down

D. L. Moody's preaching services because of his gluttony and obesity. The Christian will have to conclude that during the many years when Dwight Moody was daily practicing the materialistic sin of gluttony, God used this man over and over to win throngs of people to Christ! It is a tribute to Christians of Moody's time that they did not permit his gluttony and obesity to prevent them from seeing his many good and positive qualities. This has a lesson for marriage, for blessed are the husband and wife who are able to overlook certain weaknesses of the flesh and imperfections in one another if in doing so they are able to see and appreciate their many good qualities. Not every conflict in marriage can be overcome. In many cases there is only the grace to come to terms with it, usually by setting the issue in proper perspective and focusing attention on the more positive avenues of enrichment within the marriage.

The tendency to overeat does not originate completely within an individual's body. There are objects outside the body that serve as temptations and enticements. The Apostle Paul spoke of wrestling with principalities and powers. For the Christian who is easily lured by food, much of life is indeed a battle. It will be helpful if the Chrisitan can see clearly that there is a war going on against enemies called "calories" and "cholesterol." But to do battle solely in order to make oneself feel righteous may be not only ineffective, but self-defeating. What is needed is a carefully devised strategy with effective tactics. For those who feel that they are prepared to work at reforming their eating habits, I recommend that they consult the pages listed under "Weight loss" in the index of the book *Self-Directed Behavior* by David Watson and Roland Tharp.[5] The authors of this book offer behavioristic tactics for the individual to use in developing sensible eating habits. There are many other books and programs available for the warrior who is determined to strengthen his defense against the temptations of food. I would encourage such a warrior to enlist the help of trustworthy friends and relatives in doing battle with the calories. Also at the family conference, one's spouse and children can be asked to help in mapping out the battle plan and implementing the tactics against overeating. The book *Self-Directed Behavior* may be looked upon as a battle manual, and it is refreshing to know that people can be helped to fight against temptations rather than to make war on one another.

Adultery as Weakness of the Flesh

I want to speak of another minister, who for many years served as an effective Christian preacher. Jeremy Franklin (I will not use his real name) was the pastor of a large church noted for its strong evangelistic thrusts and witness. Franklin was himself an outstanding preacher, so much so that other pastors used to invite him to lead services in their churches. He was known as a man of God who through his powerful preaching could reach people of all walks of life for Christ.

But one day the news leaked out. Jeremy Franklin, a married man for many years, had for years been having a steady affair with a woman outside his church. His wife knew of it but did not wish to divorce her husband. Upon learning of the affair, the church people and ministers demanded that Franklin cease the affair immediately. To make the story short, the pressures became so great and the issue so heated, that Franklin resigned his church, left the ministry, and divorced his wife, who had been humiliated by the publicity.

D. L. Moody was unable to give up his gluttony, but the churches nevertheless accepted his ministry from the Lord even though they disapproved of gluttony. Jeremy Franklin was unable to give up his adultery, but the churches could *not* accept his ministry while at the same time disapproving of his adultery. When Franklin divorced his wife, he certainly did not cease to be guilty of living in a condition of the sin of adultery. For, lest we forget, except in limited cases, to live as a divorced person is in the eyes of God to live in a *condition* of adultery. I wish, therefore, to raise a few very disturbing questions: Might it not have been better had the churches refrained from pressuring Jeremy Franklin into his drastic decision? Could they not have informed him of their strong disapproval without rejecting completely his ministry if he could not take their advice? Is it really better that

Franklin is now no longer leading numbers of people to Christ? If God could work through Dwight Moody despite his gluttony, as well as through other ministers despite their sins of jealousy, strife, dissension, and the like, then why should we doubt that God could have continued working through Jeremy Franklin despite his practice of the sin of adultery by having the affair? Moody never found the grace to learn to eat with temperance, and Franklin may never have found the grace to cease his affair with the woman. But is it really biblical to assume that God could work through Moody and his weakness of the flesh but not through Franklin and his weakness of the flesh?

My fundamental concern here is to argue a rather conservative case for keeping marriage going whenever possible. It seems that divorce can too often be one of the most radical and devastating of human experiences for all concerned. It may be that out of motives of compassion, Christians have too easily come to view divorce as *the* "socially acceptable" form of adultery. What I suggest is that in some cases, although not all, the children and the spouse alike would be hurt much less if an affair were tolerated or accepted (without approval), just as Moody's gluttony was tolerated (without approval). This is not in the least to say that either gluttony or adultery is to be sanctioned. Rather, it is to say that in some cases it is wise to choose to live with the lesser of two evils. In Jeremy Franklin's case, he moved from one style of adultery into another by giving up his affair and divorcing his wife. Christians need to ask themselves whether divorce is always the least harmful form of adultery. Perhaps there is another form which, while sinful in God's eyes, is at the same time less humanly destructive than divorce might be. If there is, then might not this option be preferable to divorce? I hope that my readers will appreciate what I am concerned with all along in this section, namely, *to avoid whenever possible the destructive and radical step of divorce.*

If the above paragraphs are disturbing to you, you might read again some of the sins that Paul mentioned in Galatians 5: 20-21: strife, jealousy, anger, selfishness, envy, party spirit, etc. These are all classified as "the works of the flesh." If you are guilty of any one of them, you are in the eyes of God *a trans-gressor of the whole law of God.* This thought should make you at least more willing to think seriously about the above paragraphs. In the same epistle in which he listed these sins of the flesh, Paul also offered the following injunction: "For if any one thinks that he is something, when he is nothing, he deceives himself." (Gal. 6:3)

It may sound strange to some sincere believers to hear that to be guilty of one sin is to be guilty of violating the *whole* law of God. But that is what the New Testament teaches. To be sure, this teaching is very hard for the natural mind to take, but the evangelical Christian is bound to accept the teachings of the New Testament. In order to gain some perspective on adultery, we must look at some important biblical passages.

All Transgressions Are the Same in God's Eyes

Although a small percentage of Christians profess to have reached a state of perfection, most admit that they continue to sin. There is no point here in raising the question of *which* particular sins are committed most by Christians today, for according to the Epistle of James, all sins are in some sense the same in the eyes of God.

> For *whoever keeps the whole law but fails in* one *point has become guilty of* all *of it. For he who said, "Do not commit adultery," said also, "Do not kill." If you do not commit adultery but do kill, you have become a transgressor of the law. (James 2:10 R.S.V., emphasis added)*

Now, most Christians do not commit overt acts of adultery or murder, although in times of war they may through soldiers contribute indirectly to these transgressions. Be that as it may, James stated bluntly, "But if you show partiality, you commit sin, and are convicted by the law as transgressors ." (James 2:9 R.S.V.) There is little doubt that many Christians do show partiality, that is, discrimination, in favor of the rich over the poor.

James in his epistle certainly believed that some of the Christians to whom he was writing had been guilty of discrimination and were therefore guilty of transgressing the whole law! In our society, in which advertisement is a permanent part of the social environment, it is doubtful that very many Christians can go through an entire week without committing the sin of coveting. And if we accept what James has written, we must conclude that perhaps most Christians in our society are guilty of transgressing the whole law at least every week. Indeed, when we take into consideration the sins of omission, it is doubtful that any Christian goes a day without sinning. In the words of James, "Whoever knows what is right to do and fails to do it, for him it is sin." (James 4:17 R.S.V.)

If I understand what James was saying in his epistle, then I must conclude that in the eyes of God there is a sense in which there are *no degrees of sin*. Adultery, gluttony, murder, coveting, failing to do what one ought to do, showing partiality or discriminating against people, and bearing false witness are equally sinful in God's eyes; for to be guilty of *any one* of them is to be guilty of *all*. When a person is rejected in a job because of color of skin, then in the eyes of God the racist employer is no less guilty of transgressing the entire law than if he had slept with his neighbor's wife or stolen money from his father.

In order to understand the biblical implications of gluttony and adultery, we may consider the following: Mr. Adams is dismissed from his church because it is learned that he regularly has sexual intercourse outside marriage. Mr. Martin, on the other hand, is allowed to remain a member and to hold office in the church even though he is known to be guilty of the sin of gluttony. If I understand the biblical view of gluttony and adultery, then I am compelled to conclude that there is no biblical ground for dismissing Mr. Adams (the adulterer) without at the same time dismissing Mr. Martin (the glutton). This doubtless is a disturbing conclusion for many of us, but we must admit that sometimes the Bible does overturn some of our preconceived notions.

We must follow honestly this train of thought by asking the

very painful question: should D. L. Moody's church have dismissed him from membership because of his regular practice of the sin of gluttony? We must not pretend that this outstanding evangelist was not really gluttonous. This raises again the serious question as to whether churches should decline to work with a fellow Christian if he is practicing adultery. Once again, the evangelical Christian will have to admit that there have been evangelists who, while regularly practicing adultery, were nevertheless used by God to win many men and women to Christ. It would be dishonest, or at least naive, to deny this to be the case.

The Apostle Paul, in very strong words, condemned along with adultery such sins of the flesh as strife, jealousy, anger, selfishness, dissension, party spirit, and envy. (See Galatians 5:20f.) Did the apostle, then, seek to put a stop to their preaching? To the contrary, he rejoiced that at least Christ was being preached even if by the mouths of those guilty of envy. (See Philippians 1:18.)

The Apostle Paul, in very strong words, condemned along with adultery such sins of the flesh as strife, jealousy, anger, selfishness, dissension, party spirit, and envy. (See Galatians 5:20f.) Yet we know that many effective Christian workers have not overcome all these sins. Many people even offer prayers of thanksgiving for the way God works mightily through Christians who are guilty of sins of the flesh. Indeed, the Apostle Paul himself noted that out of the sin of *envy* some of his contemporaries preached Christ. (See Philippians 1:15.) Did the apostle, then, seek to put a stop to their preaching? To the contrary, he rejoiced that at least Christ was being preached even if by the mouths of those guilty of envy. (See Philippians 1:18.)

The Practice of Spouse Blaming

On the question of adultery, I wish to make a few more observations. In counseling with married men and women who have committed adultery, I have observed the following. When involved in an experience of adultery, some people tend to feel obliged to find as many flaws in their spouse as they can. I think that in many cases they are trying to make their adultery justifiable. "After all," so the story goes, "my wife doesn't appreciate me, isn't sexually responsive, isn't . . . and so on."

What I suggest is that we need not go blind and irrational when we talk about adultery. God has not given us the spirit of fear and hysteria. The cold fact is that the churches are not going to eliminate all adultery from the face of the earth or even from their own rolls, any more than they are going to clean all dissension, party spirit, strife, and jealousy out of the churches! What I am suggesting is that adultery can be dealt with both biblically and with practical worldly wisdom. When counseling with adulterers or adulteresses, I do not encourage the practice of talking about the flaws of the counselee's spouse. Sometimes I say very frankly something like the following: "Look, you ought to admit that you are engaging in adultery because you *want* to. It gives you pleasure. These attempts to make your spouse look like a monster are largely a cover-up for your own desires."

If you yourself are given to jealousy or strife or overeating, then perhaps you can understand someone who finds it practically impossible to give up—at least in the very near future—his or her affair. You feel that God forgives you even though you are not in a state of perfection regarding the sins of anger, gluttony, envy, or certain other sins. And so, may God forgive the Christian who is having an affair even if he or she cannot yet give it up and cannot help wanting the affair? Indeed, if you overeat, you want the excessive food and yet you do *not* want it. By the same token, a Christian who is involved in adultery may be in inner conflict—just because he is a Christian. If he were not a Christian. he might not *want* to give up his adultery. And yet as a natural man he *wants* to engage in the adulterous affair. The Apostle Paul certainly understood the inner conflict when he wrote, "For I do not do what I want, but I do the very thing I hate." (Rom. 7:15 R.S.V.) We ask, why did Paul do what he hated? Because as a *natural* man he *wanted* to do it.

I am not writing for Christians who claim to be perfect. Rather, I have in mind those who, like Paul, sometimes do things that they do not want to do. Yet Paul, despite his lack of perfection, regarded himself as fully within the circle of God's grace.

I wish to say very frankly that a man or woman may stand within the circle of Christian grace even though he or she is committing adultery. That is, the person may be involved in this sin and experience profound forgiveness. If it has become a habit that the individual has not yet triumphed over, he or she does not cease to be a Christian, any more than you cease to be a Christian when you give in to anger or manifest jealously or strife.

The Practical Side of Morality

I have shown that, biblically speaking, adultery, envy, strife, gluttony, and the like are in some respects all alike in God's eyes. But morality is also a matter of practical human relationships on earth. The Sabbath, said Christ, was made for man and not man for the Sabbath. Hence, it might be that on one level adultery and gluttony are alike, whereas on the level of practical relationships among people they are quite different. If this is indeed the case, then a person might say that he or she would much prefer to have a spouse guilty of strife or gluttony than a spouse guilty of adultery. Apparently this is how D. L. Moody's wife felt. She was prepared to accept and love him despite his sinful gluttony. I do not know whether she would have accepted him had he been guilty of adultery.

On the other hand, I think many Christians are perhaps a bit too presumptuous when they think that *every* Christian would prefer his or her spouse to be a glutton (or to be full of strife or envy) than to be having an affair. We are compelled by evidence to admit that strife and gluttony can easily take years off a person's life. There are some Christians who would rather have their spouse alive and healthy—even if he or she is having an affair—than to watch the spouse's blood pressure accelerate abnormally because of gluttony or strife. Gluttony, strife, and obesity need not lead to a premature death, but the chances for death are increased considerably by either gluttony or strife.

I am trying here to place adultery in practical perspective. Some marriages have to go on in the face of the threat of a sudden heart attack brought about by gluttony or strife. Other marriages have to go on even though adultery is being practiced by at least one partner. No one can say absolutely which is the lesser of the two evils.

It is perhaps now a bit clearer than it was before that there is much more to be said on this topic of adultery. And that is a major purpose for my writing about it in this chapter. It is my hope that thoughful Christian leaders will carry on this dialogue further than I have developed it here. There is nothing to be gained by pretending that the problem of adultery will go away or that we can avoid having to make sometimes very complicated decisions regarding it.

If Your Spouse Has an Affair

If you have good reason to think that your spouse is having an affair, there is no need to suppose that there is only one approach to use in coming to terms with the situation. You are not biblically bound to tell your spouse that unless he or she gives up the affair, you will leave. As I noted much earlier in this chapter, it *may* even be that you have no biblical right to do this. If you divorce your spouse on this ground, you may yourself be committing adultery in God's eyes. It is true that our society would not count it as adultery against you, but I am trying to speak strictly from a biblical point of view. Sometimes Christians take up views that they think are Christian but which are not clearly biblical at all.

When Ruth Arnold learned that her husband was having an affair, she went through a period of depression in which she allowed her faults as a wife and mother to loom to the foreground. Her good qualities were pushed into the background. When a traumatic experience happens to us, we sometimes become susceptible to excessive self-blame and thoughts of inferiority and worthlessness. That is what happened to Ruth. It never occurred to her to think that perhaps her husband Charles, finding himself attracted to another woman, simply was too lacking in self-control to prevent the affair from developing. For some curious reason, our society sometimes seems to assume that because a man *ought not* to become attracted to two women, he therefore *cannot* do so. But this is an erroneous assumption which Christians cannot afford to make. There are many occasions in which people *can* do what they *ought not* to do. If this were not the case, there would be no need for moral laws.

The simple fact is that Charles Arnold cared very much for his wife Ruth and was strongly attracted to her. He *also* became strongly attracted to Sheila. But instead of admitting that he could be attracted to two women, Charles unconsciously felt that he had to find fault with his wife in order to relieve his guilt for developing an affair with Sheila. As a Christian, Charles knew that to engage in adultery was to violate the seventh commandment. But instead of admitting to himself that he lacked the strength to constrain his attraction to Sheila, he began to rationalize that his wife was not living up to her marital agreement.

Because we finite mortals are always imperfect, it can always be said of those of us who are married that we have faults. This is especially true if the marital standards are exceedingly high. Nevertheless, there is no denial that the marital commitment does have standards of expectation. If you believe that your spouse has unjustifiably fallen below those standards, you as a Christian are under moral obligation not to use this as an excuse for developing an affair. Rather, if your spouse has fallen much too short of your marital standards, then this must be taken as a signal telling you to begin doing what is required to strengthen and improve the marriage. Much of this book is devoted to suggestions for doing just that.

When Ruth learned that her husband Charles was having an affair, she did not need to conclude automatically that she was a very bad wife. Charles simply allowed his attraction to Sheila to develop when as a Christian he ought to have exercised self-discipline. Charles was strong in spirit, but weak in the flesh. There is nothing Christian on Ruth's part if she irrationally begins to heap blame upon herself. Christianity is not a faith that generates blame and guilt for their sakes. When an affair is discovered, it may indeed be appropriate to look in depth at the marriage. But it need not be a time of morbid self-incrimination and hasty decisions.

How to Deal with Your Spouse's Affair

Drew Sloan and his wife Lena had been active church members for years. It was hard for Drew to accept that Lena was having an affair with another member of the church. But it was true, and Drew now knew it to be true. He asked himself what he should do. Should he say nothing and hope that the affair would burn itself out? Statistically speaking, most of them do. The Apostle Paul offered the following advice:

> *Brethren, if a man is overtaken in any trespass, you who are spiritual should restore him in a spirit of gentleness. Look to yourself, lest you too be tempted. (Gal. 6:1 R.S.V.)*

No doubt, this advice applies equally to a woman overtaken in a trespass. If Paul's recommendation is taken, then Drew cannot go to Lena and demand that she give up the affair. That would not be approaching her "in a spirit of gentleness." If adultery is seen as a weakness of the flesh, then we may find it not very practical to attack the adulteress herself, for that could make her even weaker. Let us ask ourselves: what steps should Drew take? He is perfectly within his rights to tell Lena that the affair is a serious failure to live up to the marital standard. But this is not the same as telling her that she has broken a contract, for that implies that Drew is now free to do as he wishes now that the contract has been invalidated.

This deserves a more profound treatment. In the first place, Christian marriage is certainly more than a contract between two people. It is a commitment of depth which, from a Christian perspective, involves God, the human community, and the children (if there are any). In the second place, because Christian marriage is not a mere contract, it is not made automatically invalid by an affair. Even if Lena lacks the strength to give up the affair for the time being, Drew does not have an absolute and unconditional justification for initiating a divorce. To be sure, in the eyes of the state he does. But we are here dealing with the biblical and Christian dimensions of marriage and not merely the legal angles.

Of course, if a person enjoys the theatrics of an old-fashioned showdown, then he or she may demand that the affair be ended immediately. In some situations this may prove to be an effective approach. But it is necessary to understand that each marriage is unique. What may prove effective in one may result in disaster for another. What may bind and heal in one may make deeper wounds in another.

Indeed, there is no rule that guarantees that the tough line will bring better results than will patience. Very often a marriage survives an affair simply because the partner who discovers the affair does not make a test case of it. A wife may strongly disapprove of her husband's gluttony. She may resent his becoming fat, especially if she tries to take care of her own appearance. She may realize that in overeating, her husband is increasing the chances of dying and leaving her a widow with the children to raise. But in this situation she need not throw down an ultimatum. Rather, with patience and skill she may work with him in the spirit of gentleness to strengthen him so that he can resist excessive food. Similarly, Drew need not throw down an ultimatum, but may, instead, patiently do what he judges will be effective in helping Lena to curtail her affair eventually. He might, for example, endeavor to make their marriage even more interesting. Or he might simply wait patiently with reasonable confidence that what he and Lena have developed in their relationship over the years will be more than strong enough to extinguish the affair in time. When the Apostle Paul listed the fruit of the Spirit, he did not include panic on the list.

Drew may recommend to Lena that if she cannot yet give up the affair, then she would do well to be discreet. This in no way sanctions her sin, but it does recognize some of the practical problems involved in living in a human community. There are children, relatives, and friends to think of. Drew's self-respect and strength during this experience may very well cause Lena to gain a new appreciation of her husband and to appreciate him in a way that she never before has.

Sex Is not a Magical Act

Of course, sex in our society has been made into all sorts of things. Many people still see it as a kind of pagan magical act. Some men think that if their wife has sex with another man, then she is like a piece of used goods or property. I cannot stress strongly enough that this attitude is unchristian. In the first place, neither a woman nor a man is a piece of goods. In the second place, adultery is the abuse of a perfectly wholesome act, just as gluttony is the abuse of the wholesome act of eating. Adultery is sinful because it is using a good experience in an inappropriate manner.

When D. L. Moody was gluttonous, he was not defiled in some magical sense. And when Lena committed adultery, she was not defiled in this magical sense. Rather, she gave her sexuality in the wrong relationship. Hence, Drew, instead of thinking of his wife as somehow "stained" in some weird magical sense, would be more accurate to see what the problem really is. She is misdirecting her affections and her sexuality. Drew's commitment is to work skillfully with her to see that their Christian commitment entails that sexuality be confined to marriage in order to enrich and strengthen the marriage and to make it more meaningful.

Drew may have been neglecting Lena. But we must resist the tendency to think that if an affair is taking place, then something *must* have been wrong with the marriage. Granted, this is a common assumption, and in some cases it is justified. But in many cases the affair means two things: (1) a new phenomenon has affected the marriage in some way, and (2) some wise and effective plan is required to deal with the new phenomenon. By looking at the affair this way, Drew does not necessarily have to ask, "Where have I gone wrong?" Rather, in a more positive and constructive frame of mind he can ask, "What can be done to help our marriage to grow and be interesting to both of us?" Indeed, even if Lena had *never* committed adultery, Drew would have done well to ask himself this question periodically. While there is no way to guarantee that one's spouse will never have an affair, there are ways to strengthen and enrich a marriage so that it may place an affair in perspective and not be swamped by it should it happen.

How to Begin Communicating

Even if your own spouse has never had an affair, you may be called upon by a friend or relative to offer your judgment on what he or she should do in the case of an affair in the family. In short, you may be called upon to help save a marriage. You might be asked this question: "I know that my husband is having an affair, but should I tell him that I know?" Or you might be asked another question, "My husband knows that I know about his affair, but how do I bring it up for discussion?" Let us begin with the second question. We will give your imaginary friend a name—June.

We will keep in mind that the following is one approach that is in keeping with the Christian spirit.

June tells her husband that she wishes to talk with him. After a time is arranged and she has made certain that her husband is in fact having an affair, she begins:

> I know that you are having an affair, Kevin. I know also that we have been good for each other in our marriage. It has been very meaningful to me, and I desire very much that it continue to be. I cannot accept this affair as right, but I do not intend to panic over it. I will trust you to make no hasty decisions.

Kevin, after recovering his balance somewhat, will likely say something. June must listen very attentively and patiently, giving Kevin time to speak, and try to avoid outbursts and reckless charges.

June speaks again:

> I know, Kevin, that even after the marriage ceremony we sometimes find other people attractive. We do not go blind just because we get married. I can't deny being tempted myself. We are both human. All I want to say is that I love you very much and I believe that your love for me has

been genuine and sincere. This affair does not make you into a monster. On the other hand, I do not expect to be thought of as a wife who lacks understanding. I have always appreciated you and plan to appreciate you in many other ways in the years to come. I believe you have appreciated me in many ways. This affair cannot change that fact. If you wish now or later to talk about this matter, just say the word. I have a good ear. I will, of course, trust you not to embarrass me by being indiscreet.

Let us look at June's approach very briefly. First, she assured Kevin that she would not use the affair as a cause to destroy the marriage. Second, she assured him of her own positive feelings toward him. Third, she stated her postion that she could not approve of the affair. Fourth, she made it clear that she expected Kevin to show her respect. In short, she was teaching him how he may respond positively to her in this trying situation. She was willing to understand and to work with him, but she was not willing to be made a scapegoat.

There are some things that a particular husband and wife simply are unable to talk about—at least not yet. Forgiveness and mutual acceptance does not always have to be communicated by words. June may decide that she and Kevin lack the communication skills to discuss his affair. But desiring *eventually* to arrive at the point when they can discuss it, she may very patiently begin now working to improve her communication with Kevin on *other* subjects. This in itself could enrich their marriage. In a later chapter, I will offer some suggestions on how to develop the skill of listening. In dealing with an affair or any other threat to a marriage, a good rule to follow is to start with what we do very well, to show respect for our spouse, and to elicit respect in return.

It is wise to keep the affair in perspective. From the Christian perspective, it is a sin, but it is not the unpardonable sin. It is a weakness of the flesh and need not be regarded as an aggressive act. It can, of course, be accompanied by aggression and hostility if the adulterer thinks that he or she has to blame the spouse in order to justify the affair. June would be wise indeed to regard Kevin's adultery, not as a deliberate attempt to show disrespect for her, but as simply his own weakness of the flesh and lack of self-control. In my own judgment, psychiatrists have made far too much of the mother-hatred and wife-hatred theme in male adultery. The biblical position is more realistic. It declares adultery to be basically a failure to limit one's passions and sexual interests to the marital bond. The wise person will look for positive and constructive ways to keep marriage interesting and to develop in himself or herself and spouse better controls of this healthy passion. Furthermore, the wise Christian married couple will be alert to opportunities to open their marriage, not to new sexual partners, but to new opportunities for enriching their lives with one another, both sexually and in numerous other ways. That is the Christian answer to open marriage.

VI
MARITAL OPENNESS THROUGH CREATIVE LISTENING

Is Anyone Listening?

As a boy I used to think that prayers were three things: (1) thanksgiving, (2) confessions, and (3) making requests—asking, seeking, and knocking. Not until I read the Bible for myself was I struck by another aspect of prayer—(4) *expressing negative feelings*. People in the Bible suffered a lot, and in prayers they sometimes said aloud that they did not like the way things were going. In the Bible there are prayers of complaint, disillusionment, despair, anger, and even verbal expressions of vengeance and violence. Some of the Psalms sound as if they are transcriptions from a hard and bitter therapy session, when the client is at rope's end and is fed up with life in general. Some therapy sessions can be pretty expressive and explosive with anger and resentment. I remember my own shock upon reading for the first time Psalm 137. The author was angry—really angry. In fact, he was enraged. The Babylonians had pushed him and his family around long enough. He was so enraged that before God he blurted out that he wished that someone would take the little children of the Babylonians and dash "them against the rocks." (Psalms 137:9 R.S.V.)

The entire book of Lamentations is filled with expressions

of very negative feelings. Christianity teaches that God intended that these prayers of negative utterances be included as a part of sacred Scripture. It is unfortunate that some Christians have come to believe that they should not even express aloud their sense of disappointment, hopelessness, anger, or revenge. Modern psychotherapy holds that under certain conditions, giving verbal expression to negative feelings is much better than bottling them up, as it were. From the Christian point of view, because God already knows how we feel, we cannot hide our feelings from him. So it seems to follow that if it will help *us* to verbalize our disappointments and resentments, then so much the better. God is a good listener.

In one of his prayers the prophet Habakkuk was so distraught that he became very sarcastic with God. In essence, he asked why, if God's eyes are too pure to behold evil, does he look on faithless people when they do evil and why, then, does God, after seeing this, do nothing about it! Why, Habakkuk wanted to know, does God remain silent when atrocities are being committed all around? (See Habakkuk 1:30.) It is interesting to read the book of Habakkuk, for it reminds us of a non-directive counseling session. In the entire book, God is not reported as saying anything at all to the prophet. Yet the prophet speaks on and on, and in the process, he begins to answer his own questions.

Now, suppose God had said to Habakkuk: "Behold, you shall express your feelings no more. Be silent. I will do the speaking; you listen." No, it was God's time to listen! And Habakkuk, despite all his doubts, prayed on and on because he simply believed that God was listening to him. In Habakkuk's mind, God was the most patient listener.

Everyone needs to be listened to. If you do not believe this, take a long bus ride. The chances are that if you are a good listener the person next to you will begin to pour out his or her heart to you. In my office someone once said to me, "I don't know why I'm telling you all these things about myself. I hardly know you and you hardly know me." But the point is that this person continued to talk because of the powerful need to express feeling, hopes, anger, and other human emotions. In the Bible, one thing is clear. To be a person is to talk and talk and talk. God talks to men and women; they talk to God. And men and women talk to each other. Christ is himself referred to as "the Word." "In the beginning was the Word . . . ." (John 1:1)

But is anyone listening to all this talk? In this chapter I wish to explore practical ways for husband and wife to listen more effectively to one another. In recent years much emphasis has been placed on the need to open the marriage to outside influences and interests. Along with this, however, I wish to emphasize the equally important need to develop greater openness between husband and wife. In many ways, these two emphases should always be seen as complementary and supporting each other.

In practically every marriage one spouse has at times said to the other, "You just don't hear what I'm saying. You recognize my words, but you don't understand their meaning."

I take a modest amount of pride in knowing that I listen a great deal to my wife and that she and I communicate reasonably well. But I remember in particular an experience in which I was flustered by her sincere remark that I did not understand at all her feelings or what she was saying about a certain matter between us. I had heard *other* married people say this of each other, but I had convinced myself I could not lose contact with my own wife. But in this case I clearly had! There is no point in denying that I became frightened, for I realized in a flash what a terrible thing it would be to develop a fixed pattern of listening to the one I love most and yet not really hearing her.

A good quarterback improves his passing by practicing. I asked myself if I had gradually quit practicing the art of listening carefully to my wife. Slowly recognizing the need to improve the skill of listening, I determined to hear my wife rather than simply assume that I *already knew* how she felt and what she thought on every important concern and question. I do not know where or how the notion developed that it is unmanly for a man to pay close attention to what his wife is saying. But it is a vicious notion. To be sure, there are a great number of women and men who sometimes have very little worth listening to as they ramble on as if their minds were noise transmitters.

Yet, all the same, they are human beings and not simply wind in the trees or the noise of traffic in the city. Perhaps some people pour forth an excessive amount of trivia because they have not been taught to filter out the useless noise in order to focus on their more important feelings and ideas. Thanks to recent studies of interviews between psychologist Carl Rogers and his clients, we are now able to say that creative listening can become a powerful method for teaching another person to speak more interestingly and intelligently.[1]

Creative Listening in Marriage

Creative listening is the skill of *rewarding* with attention the kind of talk that you think is important. Of course, if you are married, you first have to *want* to hear what your spouse feels and thinks about certain things. But because of time and energy limitations, a spouse simply cannot listen to just everything. He or she must select (1) what to listen to carefully and (2) what to keep in the near background. At this point creative listening becomes an art.

The second thing about creative listening in marriage is that the *listener* must act and behave in an easily recognizable way when he or she is listening attentively. This may be called *listening behavior*. This behavior must be so sharply set off from mere casual or half-hearted listening that one's spouse can quickly detect it. Surprisingly, overt *listening behavior* is not difficult to learn; it is a skill that most people already possess but often use haphazardly. What is needed, however, is a perfecting of this behavior through regular *practice*.

In their book *The Mirages of Marriage*, William Lederer and Don Jackson contend that marriage is primarily an interlocking *communication* system.[2] "The behavior and the attitudes of one partner *always* stimulate some sort of reaction from the other.''[3] The theory of creative listening works under the assumption that even the way one spouse listens to another will affect the way the other talks, what he or she talks about, and even the way he or she behaves. Of course, practically any adult could tell you that marriage runs on the rails of communication—of speaking and listening to one another. Yet why is it that so many marriages have serious and often permanent breakdowns in communication?

I think that a partial answer lies in a failure to appreciate the fact that communication is not some ethereal phenomenon but is composed of observable patterns of behavior, many of which can be focused on, broken down into details, and then practiced. This may be compared to the way that a coach uses a camera to focus on certain passing and blocking behaviors that he breaks down into precise detail, studies, and then has his players to practice until they improve considerably their performance.

The following is a set of listening behaviors that you may analyze and then put into practice in order to improve the communication and understanding between you and your partner.

a. *Move your body into a listening position.* If you judge that your spouse is trying to talk about something that is very important, then speak to him or her with your body actions. Turn your *face and eyes* in the direction of your spouse. If you have something in your *hand*, put it down or aside. Let your spouse literally *see* that you are not dividing your attention between him or her and whatever you have in your hand. It is amazing to discover how rewarding this simple act can be to someone who is talking. (Later, we see how it is also a *controlling* device that the listener can employ.)

b. *Use your eyes and head to actually encourage your spouse to continue talking on the important subject that he or she has just begun.* Raise your eyebrows and open your eyes, not enough to steal the scene, however, but just enough to let your spouse *see* that you are open in your face, which suggests that you might also be open in your mind. As your marriage partner continues to talk, nod your head, just a bit, in an affirmative manner. This is a very smooth and unobstrusive way of signaling that the conversation is still going on, that it has not been cut off, that you are focusing on what is being said. In .fact, if you have never consciously done it before, try experimenting with the power of eye-and-head-talk. Practically anyone can tell you that eye-and-head-movements are a part of conversation. But these movements can be used far more effectively than most people use them. By a careful and skillful use of your eyes and head alone, you can sometimes lead a person to tell you things that that individual never would have imagined telling you. (Needless to say, you will frustrate your own efforts if you give intimate or private information about your spouse to other people against the wishes of your spouse. Marital faithfulness entails that you do not betray intimacy! Recently a minister was fired from his church largely because he had taped, without permission, some counseling session between himself and members of his church. He even played the tapes, without permission, at a seminar. Such a violation of trust does not encourage further trust.)

c. *Improve the physical setting of your conversation.* If you judge that your spouse is beginning to say something that is extremely important, then in a quiet and unobtrusive manner guide the two of you to some area of the house where interference is less likely to occur. Or, it may be necessary simply to turn the TV off. In doing this—without interrupting—your spouse will again *see* that you care. To care for another person is not just to have a feeling. Rather it is to take care that the *objective details* of the setting and environment are properly arranged so that the personal relationship may develop unhindered.

d. *Use non-attention wisely.* If in your best judgment you decide that your spouse has for some reason begun to wander far away from the important point or feeling that was being expressed, then do not reward this excessive wandering with the forms of attention that we have considered immediately above. If your mate is wandering away from the subject, then very gently look up to the ceiling or out the window. But do not do this in any excessive manner. Be very, very slight. Why? You do not want to anger your marriage partner or call unnecessary attention to yourself. You want simply to send a very slight signal to the effect that you are not going to reward rambling and aimless talk.

There are a number of devices for communicating *nonattention*, one of the best of which is that of simply focusing your eyes on your clothes, feet, a shelf, or on practically anything other than the speaker.

e. *Quickly reward a return to the subject.* Try to avoid the old "You're-not-listening!" "Oh-yes,-I-am!" exchange. Instead, as soon as your spouse veers back even slightly in the direction of the topic of importance, then nod your head positively but gently, open your eyes in an interested way, or say, "Yes, I see" or, perhaps even better, simply grunt in an interested and attentive way. In fact, a creative use of light grunts and sounds should not be overlooked. Regard them as *shorthand* for longer expressions. A well-timed and carefully expressed grunt in the conversation can deliver a considerable amount of meaning to the speaker without interrupting. Also carefully placed silence can sometimes be helpful in creative listening.

f. *Restate or repeat some of what you hear.* Three weeks ago at a church party I talked to a woman who simply lacked some of the elementary skills of intelligent conversation. She listened with her eyes, but what she lacked was at least two things: First, she *merely* listened but did not *exchange ideas* with me. It was as if she were devoid of thoughts of her own. I might just as well have begun talking to the dining room chair or to the door knob just behind me. Second, the woman seemed not to know how to *summarize* any of the conversation, which left me wondering whether she had followed anything that I had said. One person had already remarked that conversing with this woman was like talking with a marshmallow. I now know what that means. Of course, in a counseling session it would have been useful to reward even the grunts and slight comments of the woman in order to encourage her to share her ideas without fear. But the party was not a counseling session.

If you are to communicate your attentiveness, you would do well now and then to try to give a very honest and simple *summary statement* of what your spouse has just said in the course of conversation. To be sure, this is a risky practice, especially if you have failed to follow the points that he or she has been making. In order to make sure that you in fact have understood the points, you might more frequently restate them—perhaps in different words—so that your spouse can determine whether his or her points have been grasped by you. If you have failed to grasp them, then your spouse can rephrase the points and give you another opportunity to understand them. It is a bit like working with each other in tennis to get the ball over the net for an interesting game.

Again, your own *judgment* will have to come into play here. You may judge that your spouse is talking about three or four subjects at once. Hence, you will have to select which one you think is more important and then *choose to restate and summarize the points of that particular subject.* As for the points that relate to the less important subjects, they can be temporarily ignored or left in the background.

g. *Keep yourself open to a revision of your conclusion about what is or is not the most important topic of the conversation.* One of the secrets of creative listening is the ability to focus on the primary topic without being completely unwilling to change the focus if it seems advisable to do so. A certain amount of *preliminary exploration* may be necessary before zeroing in on the topic. While listening, make a survey in your mind of the various topics that your spouse brings up. Do this before *discovering* which topic is the most important to him or her to discuss.

It is imperative here to stress the word *discovering.* A creative listener does not just invent what is interesting or important to discuss. He tries to *discover* what the other person considers to be important. As a husband listens and *follows the points* that his wife is making, *she* may in the process discover that the topic is less important to her than she had thought. She may move to a more pressing topic. Indeed, you and your spouse will sometimes discover together that there is something very important that you need to spell out and follow. But you would not have discovered this had you not sailed forth into preliminary exploration.

Normally the development of the exchange is as follows. You make a judgment as to what seems to be the important topic for your spouse to talk about. You listen creatively, and in the course of time the topic will be refined or revised. This is progress, for it means that evaluation and "value clarification" has already begun to take place at an early stage.

h. *Look for progress in resolving the problem.* There is no point in simply rehearsing a problem or complaint just to listen to it. *Creative* listening is not indiscriminate listening. It is listening with a purpose or aim. (Of course, there are times in which we *do* listen just for the pure joy of the sound and arrangement of notes.) It is important to listen to a spouse's complaint in order to learn what the nature of that complaint actually is. But when it is spelled out somewhat, the next step is to go to work on a conceived resolution. For example, if the children are not getting to bed on time and are making excuses for neglecting to carry out their responsibilities, then it may be map-making time. That is, it may be time for the mother and father to sit down and map out *their own responsibilities* in dealing with this problem. They may have to *divide the labor* between them so that one of them takes the initiative in caring for the bed-time details, while the other spouse plays a supportive role, so to speak. The wife's complaint may be that she has had the children most of the day, and now she would like her husband to take care of the primary details in this case.

The point here is that fruitless complaining must not be rewarded with attention. Usually such complaining will cease *if* we listen creatively and carefully to talk that is constructive, informative, useful, and interesting. In fact, the creative listener actually focuses on creative or constructive talk.

At a party, Martin was conversing with Karen, a child psychologist, when the hostess came by just to see how things were going. The psychologist complimented the host for inviting such an interesting guest to her party. Martin knew that she was referring to him. Yet he knew also that he had actually said very little to the psychologist but rather had listened carefully, asked some useful questions about her area of child psychology, and made a few summary statements during the conversation. It turned out that this child psychologist had a lot of profoundly interesting things to say and that Martin had listened well and had learned a lot. For him, it was a most interesting interchange even though he had contributed very little information. For Karen, the psychologist, it was interesting because Martin had heard much of what she said and had verbalized enough to indicate that some of her points had not been entirely lost. Apparently, she found his creative listening to be as interesting as he found her research into child psychology to be.

How to Make a Point by Listening Well

Over the past couple of decades my wife has, through example, taught me a lot about how to get a point across by listening. Instead of rushing in with words to interrupt and to point out the flaws in my reasoning, she will more often listen in such a way as to let me discover the flaw by myself—or almost by myself. It is a very effective device, I must confess. It is a device which allows me to hang my own arguments by the neck. Speaking from experience, I can say that when you hang your own bad arguments with your own rope, you are much more willing to pronounce them dead and to bury them. Usually my wife insists that I bury my own dead arguments, which is a way of saying that she does not wish to gloat at the funeral. One likes to get bad arguments out of sight as soon as possible without one's spouse or anyone else around to heap scorn on them.

By letting me take care of my own dead arguments without much fanfare or ceremony, my wife in effect says that what interests her are good arguments, hypotheses, and plans of action. So long as a plan is alive and thriving, it receives attention and respect. But once it falls repeatedly against the rocks of experience, logic, or evidence, then it is time to either revise the plan thoroughly or else bury it quickly. Beyond a point, trying to breathe new life into dead plans and hypotheses becomes a process of rationalizing and face-saving. Blessed be the woman who does not try to make her husband die emotionally with his dead hypotheses, plans, or ideas! We all have been around those necrophiliacs who sneer at us when our view or opinion has proved to be wrong. They act as if something were wrong with *us*, as if somehow *we* had fallen along with our fallen opinion and view.

Once it occurred to me that I think more creatively among those of my family and friends who allow me to have some distance between (1) the views that I sometimes set forth and (2) my own personhood. While these friends and family members may be very quick to challenge my *views* in one way or another, they do not completely identify my own personal being with the views that I set forth. Seemingly, it does not often occur to them to say, "*You* are wrong!" They are much more likely to say that my *view* is wrong and even show me *where* it is wrong. Some are quite direct in telling me that I have erred, whereas others are more indirect. The latter patiently help me to make the discovery of error more on my own and to verbalize the error myself. Blessed indeed is the person whose spouse does not insist that he eat his own words!

It is safe to say that by listening creatively and skillfully as I have plodded through plans or ideas, my wife has led me to see the points that she wanted to make. The noted psychologist Carl Rogers used to refer to his kind of therapy as "non-directive therapy." But that is very misleading. It would better be called "therapy through creative and skillful listening." Somewhere, the psychologist B.F. Skinner is recorded as telling the following story about the non-directive therapist Carl Rogers. One day Dr. Rogers went duck hunting. After finally spotting some flying ducks, he took aim and shot. At about the same time some men nearby shot at the same birds. All the men arrived at about the same time where the dead ducks were lying on the ground. The men insisted that the ducks were theirs, rather than Rogers'. Whereupon, Rogers began to restate their claims and to hear them out slowly and carefully. To make the story short, Rogers walked away with the ducks! That is creative listening. Needless to say, no one can promise that we will always walk away with the ducks, or that we ought to, if we use creative listening. Rather, the point is that creative listening does affect and influence persons with whom we interact. And, of course, if we listen, to the extent of following what our spouse is saying, then there is the genuine possibility that in *understanding* what is said, we will modify some of *our own* thinking, attitudes, and behavior. That is part of the meaning of openness in marriage.

Open Marriage and Divorce

In many ways, a discriminating openness in marriage may very well be the best way of outflanking divorce. I say this with the realization that the authors of the famous book *Open Marriage* are now divorced! The fact is that divorce strikes down so-called open marriages and closed marriages without respect for either.

Some profound *changes within* the style of one's marriage may be less traumatic and more creative than the drastic exchange called divorce. Some people divorce but never change their style of marriage from one marriage to another. Again and again they run through the same mistakes with different marriage partners. The script is the same; only the players are different. Frances Case had three husbands; but, for her, each of them was simply a slightly modified edition of that suspicious category called "man." In her mind, no husband was really greatly different from any other. She subscribed to the generalization that "all men are alike." Frances exchanged husbands, but there was never any significant growth *within* any of her marriages.

Dan and Julie Webster seemed in their marriage to have stepped onto a down-hill streetcar that could not be stopped. They were both professional people, intelligent, and far above average in looks. They loved their children and were, from all appearances, very good parents. Today Julie and Dan are divorced. Dan has remarried, but the record he is playing in the new marriage is the same one that he was playing when married to Julie. It is unlikely that the new marriage will last. What Dan and Julie needed was not a divorce, but a revision and renegotiation of some of the patterns of their marriage. They needed a change that meant growth, not an exchange of one player for another.

This is not to say that their old style of marriage was not a good and meaningful one for a number of years. Rather, it is to say that the marriage failed to grow and develop. On earth, the circumstances and conditions of living often change, sometimes drastically. It is pagan Stoicism, not Christianity, which insists that an individual remains completely the same regardless of conditions and circumstances. Because a marriage is constituted of individuals, it does not thrive irrespective of changing conditions. Rather, in order to thrive together, the married couple must communicate well what is of high value to them in their marital union and then seek to come to terms with the shifting conditions. This will normally help keep alive those values that they together have agreed to be committed to.

In the Second World War some of the French generals simply lacked the ability to communicate with their fellow officers. The results were disastrous. Marriages are sometimes at war with genuine threats from without. It is imperative, therefore, that husband and wife, in their joint defense against the threats, keep themselves open so that they can communicate their plans and be informed about their own expectations and their resources to fulfill the expectations. Perhaps if they can keep in practice at listening creatively, they will not end up making an all-out and destructive war on each other.

VII

THE
GREATEST OF THESE
IS LOVE

Misconceptions from Childhood

In his famous discourse on love in 1 Corinthians 13, Paul the Apostle writes, "When I was a child, I spoke like a child, I thought like a child, I reasoned like a child; when I became a man, I gave up childish ways." (1 Cor. 13:11 R.S.V.) It is profoundly significant that both psychoanalysts and proponents of transactional analysis regard many of our serious personality conflicts to be the direct result of failing to outgrow certain early childhood misconceptions about ourselves and others. As a little girl, Sarah thought that her father knew the answer to just about every important question, that he was never disturbed by anything that happened, and that he could do most things worth doing. When Sarah married David Todd, she seemed to assume that her husband would be pretty much what she had imagined her father to be.

As the marriage continued, Sarah felt increasingly "disappointed with the marriage." David felt both that he had been betrayed and that he himself was betraying his wife. Clearly, he was not living up to her expectations. Steadily the marriage unraveled as each new expectation brought in new disappointments.

David could not please Sarah, who began increasingly to sound like David's nagging mother.

A brief analysis of this relationship—which, incidentally, is not an uncommon one—will throw considerable light on the question of what marital love is and is not. In his courtship days with Sarah, David had passed himself off as a kind of Jack Armstrong, the All-American Boy. Contrary to the religious upbringing that she had received at church, Sarah began to worship and idolize David and to look up to him as if he were almost a Greek god, which is the way she had looked up to her father. When David gave Sarah flowers and gifts, she tended to shift into the role of Daddy's Little Girl receiving gifts from her matchless father. Increasingly, David tried to behave as Mr. Big, and Sarah rewarded this behavior by assuming the role of the little girl looking up to Mr. Big.

But in the course of time and in the real world outside the Land of Make-Believe, David did not prove to be Jack Armstrong. To be sure, David Todd was no slouch. He had talents, skills, and a pleasant disposition. But compared to Jack Armstrong and Sarah's idolized father, David looked like Don Knotts in the ring with Muhammed Ali.

In relating to David, Sarah seemed to move back and forth from acting like Daddy's Girl to playing the role of a criticizing parent to David. This pattern became more thoroughly established as David, in turn, responded to Sarah's "parenting" as if he were a little boy. This response then created in Sarah a new contempt for her husband, who was supposed to be her he-man, not a little boy. While Sarah's expectations were unrealistic, David's actual performances were only human. Practical realism in the sense of realistic expectations between this husband and wife seemed never to take firm root.

To Think as an Adult

The Apostle Paul realized that profound love requires adulthood, that is, a relationship of mutuality in which neither member of the relationship functions primarily as either parent or child to the other. A successful marriage also distinguishes child-like joy from childishness. The former is healthy and delightful zest in work and play. But the latter is the tendency to cheat in the realm of thinking. In games, little children will cheat when they either have not been taught a better way or have not come under certain moral and social controls. If people are allowed— or encouraged—to cheat, they will more than likely continue cheating at games and at other activities. By extension of this phenomenon, we can observe that some people act as if they were exempted from some of the basic structures of physical and social reality. They try to cheat reality.

Unfortunately, these powerful structures of reality do not simply yield to our fantasy life. In the case of David and Sarah, some of these structures eventually crushed their childish delusions. In Paul's words, whereas each of them had "thought as a child," it now became necessary to give up "childish ways." We say, rightly, that being *thoughtful* is an ingredient of the love re-lationship. But it is not enough simply to think *about* a person but to think also *rationally* and *intelligently* about the other person's needs, wants, and circumstances.

Love and Practical Realism

Practical realism is what gives substance and focus to our sentiments and feelings. Without practical realism, we would never rise above the level of aimless sentimentalism. This does not mean that in order to love we must be towering intellects. It does mean that human love, to become effective, requires a level of practical worldly wisdom that enables us to cope with daily cares and to learn from the hard-earned lessons of the experiences of ourselves and others. An elementary example of how practical realism develops is found in the child's play in the back yard. If a child crawls into the rose bush, the un-desirable consequences will themselves teach him or her to crawl or walk in a different direction. If the child learns from the experi-ence, there will be an increase in the individuals store of practi-cal realism. Fortunately, much practical realism and wisdom can in time be learned indirectly from other individuals and peoples of the world.

It seems that during courtship, many individuals of our particular culture lose a measure of their practical realism regarding male-female relationships. Doubtless, there are new biological developments that help create a vital interest in the opposite sex. But, unfortunately, our culture has not always been too helpful in leading people to use this new interest wisely. Charles says that he is "just *crazy* about Virginia." And in some ways this is quite an accurate description. His "romantic love" blinds him to many facets of practical realism.

Because evangelical Christians are strongly committed to the ideal of the life-long marriage, they would seem to be morally bound to do much more than they have to help young people make wise choices for marriage partners. A shoe on the wrong foot is a mismatch even if the shoe is well made and the foot is healthy. *Similarly*, a young Christian woman and a young Christian man may be very exemplary persons, but together as husband and wife they may make a very unhappy marriage. Christian sociologists and psychologists need to do more research and writing in this very practical area of mate selection.

The Impact of Mistaken Beliefs About Ourselves

In 1975 in London a man died because he was stung by a wasp. Or at least that is the way it seemed to the onlookers. But a careful examination of the body revealed that, in fact, the man had not been stung by a wasp or anything else. It turned out that the man only *thought* he had, which was nevertheless enough to kill him. Paul speaks of anything's becoming "unclean for any one who *thinks* it unclean." (Rom. 14:14 R.S.V., italics added) A noted psychologist writes:

> A snake perceived as poisonous has the same effect on an individual whether it is poisonous or harmless. For [Alfred] Alder, as for many other personality theorists, the mistaken beliefs acquired in early childhood "dominate the subsequent course of our existence...." Adler therefore saw psychotherapy as a procedure directed at rectifying the mistakes

or misconceptions of the patient: "We remain convinced that the cure of all mental disorder lies in the. . .process of making the patient understand his own mistakes."[1]

Many of us do not regard ourselves either as suffering a "mental disorder" or as "patients." But we do readily acknowledge that in our daily endeavors we sometimes are tripped by mistaken beliefs and deep-seated misconceptions about ourselves or others. The damage and hurt often caused by misconceptions that married partners have of each other is illustrated by the following case.

Laura Wright was in the process of profoundly modifying her relationship with her husband Burk, who recently said to her, "You have been living with me for ten years and still you don't know that I'm not a talker." In this interchange, Burk pictured himself as the strong and silent type, whereas his wife had quite a different picture of him. She felt that throughout their marriage he had talked rather freely but that now he was beginning to clam up. This kind of misunderstanding is quite common among many married couples.

Burk Wright is not, in fact, the silent type. I have myself observed him on many occasions to be quite a talker. He has always talked with me in an interesting and intelligent manner. Similarly, Laura has always talked rather freely and interestingly with me. So, it would appear either that Burk is not talking very much to Laura or that Laura imagines this to be the case.

The "picture" or "concept" that we have of people is largely a projected set of *responses* that we expect from them under certain conditions. A very useful thing about responses is that many of them can be easily observed, which means that we are not forced to talk about some deep and mysterious essence. True, people can mislead us with their responses, but we correct our misconception, not by consulting some psychological Ouija board, but by a more careful observation of their responses and the different conditions under which the responses occur.

It turns out that Burk Wright is, indeed, not responding to

Laura on certain topics that she finds desirable to discuss. She feels that nevertheless he *ought* to talk about them, for, after all, Burk is her husband! It is at this point in particular that Laura's misconception has caused her to run against a brick wall and to suffer frustration to the point of rage. By saying that Burk *ought* to talk more freely with her, Laura is setting herself up for profound disappointment. Her error lies in *unconditionally expecting* talk from Burk *regardless of the conditions and circumstances.*

The word *ought* serves to disguise Laura's attempt to dismiss the importance of noting the circumstances and conditions under which Burk talks to her. In Laura's mind, her husband is *supposed* to talk—no matter what. No conditionals! Laura demands unconditional conversation from Burk. And Burk himself even swallows a good deal of Laura's highly unrealistic outlook—with an ironic twist. He has begun thinking of himself as "someone who just does not talk." Period. Unconditionally! Both Burk and Laura are failing to acknowledge that *different responses come about under different circumstances and in different settings.* At least they are failing to acknowledge that this very elementary truth applies to their own marriage.

After pointing out to Laura that in fact her husband does converse rather freely under certain conditions, I suggested that she try thinking of herself as a major part of her husband's social environment. I pointed out further that as a significant part of his social environment, she herself had some control over whether he would talk with her. Her "assignment" now is to set up the social environment at the house so that the probabilities of his talking with her will be increased.

Laura has not yet come to observe carefully her own *responses* to Burk. She has not yet noticed how well she maneuvers many discussions between herself and Burk, maneuvers them so that an unusually high proportion of the talk between them is "marital hypochondriac" conversation. The unmistakable prelude in such a conversation may be stated in the following words: "Well, it's time to play the game called What-else-is-wrong-with-our-marriage?" In psychotherapy, a "game" contains "concealed motives which lead to the development of misconceptions." The motives are even concealed from the participants in the game.[2]

On the surface, this fruitless game appears to be quite realistic; for, after all, the couple are actually talking about their problems. But a more careful examination shows that their talk is the kind that will eventually talk a marriage to death. The practical purpose of bringing a problem into the open in the first place is not to stimulate an orgy of incrimination and useless guilt, but rather to locate more precisely the area that needs help and improvement. If a problem is not going to be dealt with, and if talking about it is simply to throw more oil on the fire, then it would be better to avoid even mentioning the problem.

A good deal of conversation between a husband and wife is normally not about their relationship with each other. Few practices would be more boring than that of a couple spending hour upon hour talking *about themselves* to one another. Ordinarily, it is more fruitful and enjoyable to make interesting plans together, to exchange stories, to develop ideas, to discuss the Bible, to talk of music, to sing together, and to speak of this and that special field of interest. It is usually more fruitful to develop together plans for meeting challenges than to complain or accuse each other endlessly. To be sure, there are times when it is advisable to bring differences and complaints out in the open. But once again, the point is to work together to find ways to deal with the problems, not to rehearse them. Merely looking again and again at the point of their conflict is to bypass apology and forgiveness when such is called for.

But Laura and Burk are unusually successful in *avoiding* a number of interesting and fruitful discussions that they could have. Laura seems eager to test out her verbal wallops and jabs. Without doubt, she is pretty good at this verbal boxing. Like any staggering victim, Burk covers himself and tries to keep out of range. He pulls in and clams up!

Laura claims that when she does open up to her husband by baring her soul to him, he only uses it against her. This "opening up" on her part serves to entice Burk back into the center of the ring so that the verbal fight can be continued. By dropping her guard and sticking her chin out, so to speak, Laura invites Burk to take a good hard verbal swing at her. It usually connects. And Laura falls back, bleeding emotionally, and complaining that she was taken unfair advantage of.

The truth is that both Laura and Burk are skilled verbal sluggers—so much so that each is beginning to buckle under the impact. Laura confesses that she has begun to grow weary of the contest and does not want to continue living in this way. She has even spoken of divorce, but a divorce would only leave her standing hip-deep in an economic swamp, to say nothing of the emotional ravages that would come to her while going through yet another divorce. Today my wife's hairdresser, who had just recently gone through a divorce, probably expressed in words what many other men and women have felt. The woman said that emotionally it would have been easier if either she or her husband had died. Laura has already gone through the divorce threshing machine and has no illusions about the grief and agony that it brings.

A Realistic Expectation

Despite the destructive theatrics that Laura and Burk frequently engage in, their marriage is not necessarily doomed. Each has some control to be utilized. Laura, for example, knows that Burk can carry on interesting and useful conversations with some people under certain conditions. What she can easily see is that *no one can be expected to talk sanely and interestingly irrespective of the circumstances and conditions.* Already she accepts this generalization. What remains is for her to acknowledge that her husband cannot realistically be made an exception to the generalization. She *cannot expect or predict* that he will talk freely unless he finds the experience to be rewarding. Why should anyone, including Burk or Laura, talk in a particular setting if doing so becomes more punishing than rewarding? Laura has acknowledged to me, and to herself, that she cannot reasonably expect or predict *herself* to engage freely in a conversation that is more punishing than rewarding. She reports that in a number of settings she herself is fearful of saying anything because of the anticipated hostile reactions from others. The hostile setting does not encourage her to talk. It now remains for Laura to see more clearly that her husband is no different in this respect from her. He, too, pulls away when the verbal knocks (even those delivered by his wife) are too hard or when the battle is unrewarding.

Constructural Approach to Marriage

Psychologist and Psychiatrist Israel Goldiamond holds that instead of treating problems of human interaction as manifestations of pathology, we might better consider them as *partial successes*. For example, until very recently, Laura enjoyed the verbal battles with Burk, and she had even developed a rather successful way of bringing them about. But in recent months she has found the fighting to be less rewarding than before. A child who wanders into a rose bush may have expected a rewarding experience; but when that expectation fails to materialize, he or she normally moves in another direction. Finding that wrangling heatedly with Burk is a punishing experience, Laura is already beginning to move in another direction.

Instead of *waiting* to see what Burk would do, Laura used to *actively* entice him into verbal battles with her. She was altogether ingenious in creating all sorts of new ways to involve him in these battles. Now, however, she has the greater challenge of *using her creative genius in finding new ways to entice him into interesting and enjoyable conversation between them.* If she is as successful in this venture as she has been in getting Burk to either clam up or insult her, then their marriage should have a bright future. The point here is that Laura already has demonstrated enormous control, power, and skill in achieving one goal. But having achieved it, she now finds that it is a worthless goal. She is beginning to formulate more realistic goals for herself as a marriage partner. She may be compared to an outstanding running back who has been shifted into a new position on the team. Sometimes a player does even better in his new position. We may hope that Laura will be at least as successful in her role as a constructive wife as she was in her old role as a destructive wife. Doubtless, like most of us, she will need some coaching and cheering now and then, for her new role will not be easy to establish.

In the previous chapter, I offered some practical steps in creative listening, which is still one of the most successful ways of bringing another person out of his or her clam shell. In high schools and colleges, students are taught how to make speeches. All sorts of organizations offer mini courses for adults who want to become successful speakers. Only a comparatively few courses are offered for lay people who wish to become creative and skillful *listeners*. But I have little doubt that an increasing number of courses will develop in the skill of "Articulate Listening" and the like. With only one or two well placed words, individuals can sometimes send another person into a rage or set him or her down in fright. With equal skill some people are able to listen in such a way as to guide others toward fruitful interchange and respectful involvements. It took years for Laura to develop and perfect her skill of enticing her husband into destructive arguments, and it will take considerable time for her to practice and perfect her new skill of creative listening and meaningful communication.

Marriage with Only Minimal Conversation

I would be among the first to admit that sometimes listening in a loving and creative manner is terribly difficult. But divorce is usually far more difficult! And if there is to be remarriage, then one's creative listening may still have to be developed eventually, even when it is sometimes painful to do so.

However, living in a relationship in which there is very little listening or talking is a genuine option for many married couples. In such a marital style, husband and wife do not expect to find in each other a very attentive or "articulate" ear. As a consequence, they are not greatly disappointed if no sparkling verbal exchange takes place between them. Furthermore, this kind of marriage does not suffer the agonies of regularly scheduled destructive arguments.

I would be among the last to criticize this particular style of marriage. Many of those who desire it are quite successful in bringing it about. They succeed in managing their schedules and activities in order to do the things together and separately that most interest them. If both husband and wife find this arrangement to be reasonably satisfactory, then what is the point of trying to change them? There is no one sweeping style of marriage that is suitable for every couple. Love has many levels, modes, and styles.

However, a crisis comes into play if either of the partners becomes unhappy with their particular style of marriage. Psychiatrists know that there are many women who are bitter over the fact that their husbands either will not or cannot have enjoyable and meaningful conversations with them. This raises a critical question, "Does the greatly discontented partner have a right to demand that both partners be discontent and miserable until the art of interesting conversation is developed by both partners?" This question deserves to be dealt with.

It may be that the dissatisfied member of a marriage could, out of love, find himself or herself a new job or new set of interests and activities, thus preventing a crisis from severely upsetting the marriage. Of course, if the satisfied partner insists on absolutely no change at all in the marriage—which might leave the other partner even more dissatisfied—then the marriage will risk cracking at its very foundations. Or at least one member of it might crack.

If no two marriages are exactly alike, and if no two individuals are exactly alike, then it is to be expected that in most marriages one spouse will probably want to engage in conversation more than the other. Furthermore, it is to be expected that a topic which interests one partner will not interest the other.

If the price of leading one's spouse to become more conversant is too high, then the wise thing might be to turn to other people, especially to those who also enjoy meaningful discourse and dialogue on particular topics. After all, it is unrealistic to think that anyone can be everything to his or her spouse. Not even God wills to be everything to everyone.

What Is Love?

The word "love" is used in a variety of ways, but we will not here attempt to connect all of them. Nevertheless, it will be helpful to offer some general statements about marital love even though each marriage has its own unique manifestation of love. I cannot pretend that everyone will accept the following as characteristics of marital love, but a great number of people will.

a. *Love is a finite venture involving both risks and commitments.* In the summer of 1975 a minister who founded a Bible college in Florida and who became its president happened to meet a young coed at the tennis court. To make the story very short, the two of them, in a flare of passion, engaged in sexual intercourse. Unable to bear the guilt, the president finally departed from the state of Florida and left behind a note telling of his desire never to be found by any of his friends, associates, or family. He had even changed his name so that neither his wife nor anyone else could find him.

Few people would say that this man should never have ventured out alone on a tennis court in the first place. Hermits and certain desert monks isolate themselves in order to avoid risks, but this is no way for most Christians to live. Christians can seek to cut down on foolish risks, but the doctrine of human finitude reminds us that no path is free of every snare. The president committed adultery, but in my judgment he may have done a greater wrong by leaving his wife and friends rather than trusting them to forgive and accept him. By leaving home, he divorced his wife, not legally, but effectively.

His wife was right to trust him alone on the tennis court, if she had no strong evidence for predicting that he would have involved himself sexually with another woman. Trust need not be a foolish and blind leap, but neither can it require absolute certainty. There is a wise trust and a foolish trust. Marriage requires the former, not the latter.

Of course, a person can be *committed* to the health, happiness, and well-being of another even in the face of overwhelming opposition. Marriage entails this kind of commitment, which is different from blind trust. By leaving his wife, the president of the Florida Bible college may have denied her the opportunity to *manifest her commitment* of steadfast love and forgiveness in the face of hard times and tribulation. If marriage is sometimes a risky venture, then we may expect that marriage partners will normally be found helping each other through the difficult times and will be forgiving each other along the way. "Love is patient . . . ," writes the Apostle Paul (1 Cor. 13:4).

b. *A loving spouse will be committed to the happiness and freedom of his or her partner.* Andy Hospers receives no pleasure or joy in the fact that his wife makes friends easily. In fact, he resents many of her friends and, in the process, deprives himself of their friendship. In this particular setting, it seems that Andy loves neither himself nor his wife.

However, if in other settings he clearly shows that he wants her to enjoy happiness and freedom, then to that degree we can say that he loves her. We seem forced to conclude that a husband or wife rarely loves the other unqualifiedly. Usually, one loves the other more under certain conditions than under other conditions. To be sure, today there is much talk of the unconditional commitment of love. Those who talk in this way are getting at something very important, namely, the need to extend the commitment to cover more kinds of circumstances. But it is probably a mistake to think that any finite human mortal could love another in any and every situation and circumstance.[3] Doubtless *perfect* mortal love entails that each spouse be effectively committed to the happiness and freedom of the other under *all* conditions. But human marriages manifest less than perfect love. Nevertheless, imperfect as it is, marriage often proves to be unexcelled as a form of profound human involvement and experience.

The previous two paragraphs suggest that the love existing between husband and wife can actually be *observed*. Whether or not *every* aspect of love is observable is a question worth debating. Nonetheless much of marital love can be observed. It is detected in the form of certain human responses taking place in very specific and practical situations. One purpose of a couple's engagement period before marriage is to give themselves many opportunities to observe each other in a variety of situations, thereby determining to what extent their behavior toward one another may be accurately characterized as love.

After marriage, as new situations invariably come about, couples may still observe whether or not loving behavior is present. Vance Witt *says* that he wishes his wife well in her new job, but speech is only a part of detectable behavior. He claims to love Sherry even in the situation of her working outside the home, but his overt behavior and responses will manifest publicly whether in fact he does love her as he says. To determine Vance's love in this situation, Sherry will have to ask such very practical questions as the following: Does he spend time with me in mapping out a concrete and responsible plan for raising our children properly while we both work? Does he carry through with his agreements in executing this mutual plan? Or does he complain abnormally about my working? Does he say complimentary things to others about my new job? Does he show any enthusiasm in asking me about my job? Or does he make sarcastic remarks to others about my working? Does Vance say encouraging things to me when my work is unusually difficult? In rare but real emergencies will he give me a helping hand with my work? Does his observable body language communicate interest in my work?

In answering these and many other such questions, Sherry can begin to determine with reasonable accuracy to what *extent* and in what *way* Vance loves her under the conditions of her work. By the same token, Vance, by asking similar questions about Sherry's responses, can literally observe Sherry's love for him. Marital love is not some mysterious gas that floats about undetected. It is very practical and concrete behavior. The same is true also of parental love. Parents who could reasonably be expected to be with their children and watch after them in hundreds of practical ways may be regarded as loving parents if they are *observed* carrying out responsible parental responses. But what of parents who, because of their own sickness, poverty, or other justifiable conditions, are unable to respond directly to their children's needs! Are they unloving parents? The answer is that even in such deprived conditions, parental love can still be detected. Parental love will be literally observed in the parents' attempts to bring about some genuine changes that will benefit their children.

For example, our only daughter is adopted, and the woman who brought her into the world realized that she and her husband lacked the means and physical strength to take care of their latest arrival. The family into which this infant was born was already much too large. But the woman, loving dearly her new daughter, did not sit by and watch the child grow up uncared for. To the contrary, she responded. She saw to it that her child was properly adopted through a qualified adoption agency. Anyone looking at and listening to this woman's actions and responses would have to say, "That woman truly loves her child!" Similarly, in critical situations we have literally observed individuals' caring for their spouses in hundreds of practical and meaningful ways. This "care-ful" behavior *is* love, or is at least a major portion of it.

But, of course, there are those situations in which an individual simply lacks the means of *directly* helping his or her spouse. In such cases, the loving individual will respond by locating those persons or resources that are more likely to be of direct help, just as the mother called on the adoption agency to be of direct help to her child. Needless to say, in marriage, the decision to help is under ordinary conditions a *joint* decision. Or at least ordinarily, a loving marriage partner would not presume to make a crucial decision on behalf of the other, inasmuch as marital love involves a commitment to the *freedom* of one's spouse. That is why *some* degree of intelligent communication of needs and desires is essential to any loving marriage of whatever style.

To say that marriage entails a commitment of each partner to the other's freedom is not to use words lightly. To respect another's freedom often requires considerable discipline. Freedom is not so simple a phenomenon as uncaring neglect. In a very practical sense, we gain a measure of freedom when we satisfy some of our wants and desires. But such satisfaction comes only if the concrete means for such satisfaction are available. A loving spouse must be committed to helping his or her partner obtain the necessary means to satisfying those desires most important to the partner.

Often a spouse can offer useful information and other concrete means. But to *offer* it is one thing; to insist that it be *put to use* is altogether something else. Sometimes a parent may have to "follow through" with his offer to a child. But the marital relationship is different. Giving helpful advice is usually a major function of many constructive marriages. But the commitment to freedom in marriage requires that the advice offered be treated by the giver as a considered *opinion* which the receiver is free to evaluate for himself. It is not easy to watch one's carefully formulated advice be set aside. But until partners learn to restrain themselves in this matter, their marriage will lack considerable freedom and mutuality. However, a person is much more likely to ask his or her spouse for further advice if it is known that the spouse will not tie strings to it and will not push its adoption.

c. A loving spouse will be strongly committed to the health and safety of his or her partner. Larry cannot bring himself to want his wife Martha to be happy in her work at the factory. He knows that she is gradually destroying her health because of the chemical pollution at her job. Many times he has tried to get her to quit, but she insists that the job is enjoyable to her.

Now, is Larry merely using the health hazard as an excuse to get Martha to quit outside work? Or does he want her not only to be happy in her work, but also to be able to work in a safe and healthy environment? One way to determine the extent of Larry's love is to observe the extent to which he tries to help

Martha locate a better job—one that will provide her not only a measure of happiness and freedom (as interpreted by *her*), but also a safer environment.

Health and safety are not ends in themselves. To be concerned for someone's health and safety *alone* is not enough to count as profound love. One may be physically healthy but very unhappy and unnecessarily restricted in freedom. Desiring strongly the happiness and freedom of one's spouse is, therefore, the *primary* test of love. Health and safety are important as a *means* to the end called happiness and freedom. But because means and ends are here closely bound together, we are reluctant to separate them. About sixty years ago a fashionable clergyman in England was told by his wife's physician that she would die if she should have another child. She already had nine children. The following year she had another and died. Certainly, today in Western society, such irresponsibility would normally be regarded as unloving and uncaring behavior. Still, even in this clergyman's case, we might admit that under certain conditions the man may have shown love for his wife, although in this crucial and critical situation his lack of loving care stands out so vividly as to make it difficult for us to take note of times when he did care for her in a loving way.

The Christian holds that humans can love God, because he first loved them. God is worshipped as the everlasting source of happiness, safety, health, and freedom. Many of the Psalms of the Old Testament express trust in God because he is seen as the secure ground of hope and happiness. If God were simply the supreme *power* of the universe, he would not be fully God, for the Bible teaches that God is love. It is not surprising that Jesus would give the new commandment that his disciples love one another, for they are seen as the ambassadors of divine love on earth. Throughout the Bible it is assumed that to love another is to be effectively concerned for that person's happiness and safety. Therefore, love is far more than a subjective feeling or a biological instinct. It must, in order to be love, include that very practical endeavor which Paul so beautifully described as "mutual upbuilding." (Rom. 14:19 R.S.V.)

d. A loving spouse manifests both objective and subjective love. Sue Jamison, a widow, enjoyed buying clothes for her two grown daughters. Unfortunately, she never consulted the daughters on the matter, never asked them what style *they* preferred or what color *they* liked. The daughters sometimes appeared to be ungrateful, which hurt their mother's feelings. "Why do they spurn their mother's love?" Sue asked herself. "Are mothers supposed to cease loving their daughters just because the daughters are grown women?"

Because the daughters loved their mother, they did not want to appear ungrateful. But, after accepting the clothes, with an outward expression of appreciation, they would not wear the clothes. This pattern continued for some time until out of love the daughters agreed that they would no longer let their mother spend so much of her hard-earned money on them when the gifts were not useful. Eventually they explained to her that her tastes were different from their tastes. The mother reacted as if her daughters did not appreciate her love. What she needed was to grasp the distinction between subjective love and objective love. The daughters genuinely appreciated the mother's sentiment and good intentions. But they could no longer pretend that they liked the clothes she bought for them. The mother's love was strong on subjective feeling, but it failed to enrich itself by feedback and by the *information necessary for doing something effectively and objectively good* for her daughters.

Animals can love their offspring by making them safe and secure in different kinds of settings. But because human beings live in such complex and diverse settings, their love for one another requires a measure of intelligence, know-how, and feedback that far excels that of any animal. In our complex world, love cannot remain a mere feeling or instinct. Therefore, it is useful to distinguish subjective love from objective love. The former is good will and good intentions, whereas objective love translates this subjective love into practical action. Objective love turns mere feeling and motivation into an intelligent inquiry into the needs, preferences, and circumstances of the object of our love. Objective love cannot arise until there is *feedback* from the one to be loved. Objective love is *fueled by* deep sentiment, but it is *embodied in* informed deeds and behavior.

Many a husband has bought his wife a dress or other clothing without having any reasonable amount of knowledge of whether she would like it. It is as if he wanted more to *feel* loving than to do something that would in fact make his wife happy. Some theologians speak of "cheap grace," and we may perhaps designate as "cheap love" the subjective love that neglects to learn from the beloved what would in fact contribute to his or her happiness and freedom. When people have needs and desires, we suffer a measure of arrogance if we think that the mere fact of our doing something or feeling something will somehow satisfy them. Needs and desires have *objective conditions* that are usually independent of either the benefactor's feelings or his uninformed deeds. Objective love looks into these objective conditions in order to *discover* what will more likely satisfy certain needs and desires of the loved one. Love without appropriate information is either mere sentiment or action that often misses the mark.

e. In a creative marriage, joy echoes back and forth between husband and wife. Love, says the Apostle Paul, is not resentful and is in fact patient and kind. (See 1 Corinthians 13:4,6.) We have all observed the morbid soul who cannot allow a benefactor to share in the receiver's you. In a marriage, this is especially destructive. If Jane gives her husband Matthew something that he enjoys, then normally Matthew would want Jane to share with him his joy. In a profoundly loving marital relationship, the one receiving does not hoard his or her pleasure. Rather than demand that the giver turn his or her back, the receiver kindly desires that the giver share in the delight. It takes love to receive a gift as a loving expression of the giver. *Love does not resent the giver's enjoyment in seeing his or her gift received with delight.* This does not mean that delight in receiving a gift should be faked. Rather it means that *genuine* delight deserves to be shared with the giver.

When husband and wife learn not only to give to one another, but also to welcome each other to share mutually in the joy of both giving and receiving, then they have actually multiplied their supply of happiness. Perhaps the best word to describe this aspect of marriage is *celebration*. It is fitting that after the marriage ceremony, there be a celebration. Fortunate are those partners in marriage who have their own regular celebrations with one another. A loving marriage, by celebrating its own victories and joys, is twice blessed.

Love Through Divorce?

Sam Ford had not been to my class in over two weeks. Eventually, I saw him on campus and went over to ask if he had been ill or was not coming to class for some other reason. In the course of our conversation, I asked if he had recently impregnated someone. His mouth fell open and he looked startled, but not innocent. He wanted to know what had told me, to which I had replied that *he himself* had, by his behavior and by some things that he had said to me a few weeks earlier. I explained that I was only making an educated guess and that I had no special powers of mind reading.

Sam claimed that he wanted to marry Bobbie, the girl whom he had made pregnant. I asked him to have Bobbie talk with me. She did come to my office, and after our talk, I asked if her parents knew of her pregnancy. They did. The next week Bobbie and her parents came to my home to discuss the matter. The mother was so irrational that my perceptive wife took her to the kitchen and fed her cookies. Later my wife commented that the mother seemed more concerned about what her neighbors and friends at the church would think than with what was best for Bobbie's welfare. Bobbie was active in her church and in fact was the church organist. She, her father, and I together discussed the options and came to a decision that we all agreed was the most suitable in this situation.

Sam, however, insisted on marrying Bobbie, but Bobbie insisted that she could not love him and was very doubtful that a marriage between them would last. Still, Sam persisted, even to the point of saying that the unborn child was his and that he had an absolute right to it. Later, Sam indicated that he was going to let it be known to a number of people that he had caused Bobbie's pregnancy. Fortunately, after two or three lengthy discussions with me, he came to agree that he was not yet capable of loving any woman intelligently as a husband and that he certainly was a long way from becoming a responsible father.

To make the story short, Sam came to realize that if he did indeed love Bobbie as he claimed, then he would do, within reason, what was for *her* benefit, rather than simply satisfy his own demand to marry her. We concluded that one of the best ways he could show his love for her was to leave the scene altogether and find a job in another town, for he would very soon be graduating from college. My own fear was that he would make Bobbie's life miserable if he should remain in the small town, for there was always the strong probability that Sam would one day let slip the fact that he had impregnated the church organist.

For a number of years, he either phoned long distance or wrote to tell me how he was doing. For a year or so he threatened suicide during the phone calls, but eventually this threat ceased altogether. He became a medic in the Air Force and the last word I had from him was that he was busy teaching a Sunday School class of children. By not marrying Bobbie, Sam revealed a considerable amount of objective love for her.

Sometimes, to marry someone is not a very loving thing to do. And I am forced to admit that under certain severe conditions to remain married is also not a very loving thing to do. I have known couples who showed love for each other by the fact that each wanted happiness, freedom, and health for his or her spouse. Each was even *committed* to the well-being of his or her spouse. But they simply were unable to carry through in a practical and skillful way with their commitment. Only in divorce were they able to find a way to realize their commitment of love. Throughout this book, I have been rather hard-nosed about divorce and have criticized the "divorcing fad," Nevertheless, I agree with Bruce Larson, who writes that divorce may be the lesser of two unfortunate alternatives under certain circumstances.[4]

If it is better to marry than to burn with passion, then perhaps it is better to divorce than to destroy the spiritual, moral, and emotional lives of one or two individuals, and perhaps injure seriously the children. Despite this concession to divorce, however, I have written much of this book with the aim of being of some help in preventing a marriage from declining to the point where divorce becomes the better of two unfortunate options.

The mainstream of Christianity has always taught that while divine love for men and women is itself perfect, it does not demand perfection from the recipients of that love. Therefore, the churches, imperfect and finite as they are, cannot with consistency demand perfection from those who in time of divorce and other crises need the churches' creative listening, encouraging words, and practical deeds. Love sometimes reveals itself at the strangest times and in the most unpromising circumstances. Perhaps that is why Paul the Apostle ranks love higher than either faith or hope. Christians today could do no better than follow this apostolic example.

VIII

THE
MYTH OF THE
COMPLETE PERSON

The Fog of Propaganda

Today there is much talk of the individual's becoming a "complete and whole person." If you are a woman, you may be strongly urged to become a "total woman." But what is a total woman? The answer seems to depend on who responds to the question. On some TV soap operas, a woman who has never been pregnant is classified as only "half a woman." If women should take seriously the propaganda of certain recent movies, they would have to believe that all a woman needs in order to become "fully a woman" is sexual intercourse with some solicitous Don Juan who thinks that his mission is to transform half women into whole women.

Some married people seem to imply that until an individual is married, he or she is lacking a basic ingredient of being human. The "natural fulfillment" of every normal person is supposed to be found in marriage. Some married people, after prophesying that the single life will bring only misery, set about to fulfill their own prophecy of doom by nagging their single friends about marriage.

In this chapter, I will call into question this entire notion of the fulfilled and completed person. More positively, what I will affirm is that an individual may have a good and meaningful life despite being less than a whole or a completed being. The myth of the complete person has like a heavy fog settled over a number of people and seriously affected their lives in a number of ways. To help disperse this fog is a major aim of this chapter.

Experience teaches us that marriage does not in fact fulfill or enrich the lives of some individuals. A few divorced people, reacting against the excessive claims about marriage, have rushed forth to proclaim that every married woman or man ought to get a divorce as soon as possible so that one and all may become a "true, individual person." On the one hand, marriage has been hailed as the "natural" course for any sane and healthy human adult, while, on the other hand, the single life has been hailed by others as the absolutely highest ideal of human fulfillment. A few of the early Church fathers seemed to think that marriage is a lowly concession to the "weakness of the flesh." They did not say exactly that marriage is for spiritual sissies, but they came close to saying it. For them, the real spiritual he-man is one who goes about his work without becoming intimately involved with any woman. One noted Latin father of the Church, Tertullian, felt that even though he had shown weakness in getting married, he should nevertheless not be so weak as to have sexual intercourse with his wife. For him, true fulfillment came in working at his churchly job and meditating on God. Everything else was regarded as a distraction to this highest fulfillment. Another Latin father of the Church, Origen, realizing that sex was not for him, chose to castrate himself in order to escape the temptations of lust.[1] Origen did not seem to identify his full manhood with sexual activity; but in the same soap operas mentioned earlier, a man who is sterile is described as only "half a man."

The "Real" Man and the "Total" Woman

Amid all the confusion, we cannot help asking, what *does* make a man a Real Man? What does make a woman a Total Woman? In many cases, various people tend to select the particular life-style which *they* prefer and then paste over it the title of "Total Woman" or "Real Man." Those who do this imply almost always that there is only one life-style that is "truly fulfilling."

There are two things held in common by all those who insist that true fulfillment or completeness of being comes *only* through their own particular life-style. Each assumes (1) that it is *possible* to be a completed person and (2) that we are in some way *required* to be totally fulfilled.

But the Christian teaching of human finitude makes it quite clear that no earthly, finite life-style brings completeness or total fulfillment. In light of both this teaching of human finitude and common-sense observations, Christians are forced to conclude that there simply are no completed persons on earth. Fortunately, this conclusion need not leave Christians hip-deep in morbid guilt and self-depreciation. Rather, they have the option to *accept themselves as incomplete persons.* It is not required of them to be wholly fulfilled, nor is it possible to be. The book *The Total Woman*[2] admonishes the woman to stay home and care for husband and children. It tells young women to plan to be subservient to their husbands, and provides various techniques for carrying out this plan. This one life-style of subservience is praised as *the* highest ideal for women. The best thing about the book is that it provides a strong counter-blow to those books that have been telling women that they are no good or are only half women if they stay at home to care for husband and children. Unfortunately, the book *The Total Woman* goes further to add a bit of propaganda of its own.

A Touch of Realism

A response needs to be made to those writers who demand that their own preferred life-style be canonized and elevated superior to all others. An effective way of dealing with propaganda is simply to point to some pertinent and relevant facts. The first fact is that no life-style is void of some serious disappointments and conflicts. Amid the propaganda about what is bad or good in marriage, Joseph W. Hinkle, head of the Family Ministry section of the Southern Baptist Sunday School Board of Nashville, wisely points out the following:

> It is unrealistic to think that love prevents conflict in marriage. Conflict is a part of living together; resolving conflict is necessary for couples to stay together. Bible truth reflect this over and over again...The Bible does not gloss over or sugarcoat problems that families faced. Neither should Christians today.[3]

The second fact useful in dealing with our propagandists is to be observed in what progagandists *do* as well as what they *say*. For example, many of those women who insist that subservience to the happiness of their husbands is the only way of female fulfillment are in reality pursuing careers and semi-careers of their own. While *talking* of subservience, they are actually writing books and articles and are traveling hither and thither making speeches and becoming involved in a movement of some sort outside the home. They talk subservience, but they do not practice it in every respect. To complicate the matter, what one woman writer defines as "subservience" may not be so defined by another. These women seem to relate to their husbands in various ways and then each simply labels her own way as "subservience."

Women and Work

For a great number of women and men, there are very few opportunities for them to develop *careers*. About all they can find are jobs that pay them money for helping with the fuel and grocery bills and keeping the kids' teeth in repair. Far from being fulfilling, many jobs are boring and unpleasant. For many women, a job outside the home is about as fulfilling as having a cold.

The point here is very simple even though a number of magazines and book writers seem to have overlooked it. The point is this: because individual human beings sometimes have quite different interests and backgrounds, no one kind of work could possibly fulfill or satisfy everyone. For Susan Royce, there are indeed advantages to getting out of the house and meeting a number of interesting people—*if* that is what she wants. But Susan may be much more informed than some of the women's lib people have realized. She may know that while there are some interesting people at the office, there are also a lot of *un*interesting and neurotic people, as well as many insensitive bosses. Susan may simply wish to be more selective regarding whom she associates and works with. If she is reasonably happy in working successfully as a homemanager, then what is the point in telling her that she *needs* to be somewhere else? She needs to be elsewhere only *if* she has certain interests of her own which she cannot satisfy without working outside the home or going back to school.

It is easy to point out that the job of homemanagement is unfulfilling. This is partly because practically *every* job is unfulfilling in some of its aspects. I happen to have one of the most interesting jobs in the world—for *me*. But it would satisfy most people for perhaps no more than four or five weeks. So, what *is* the greatest job in the world? The answer is that there is no such job because people are so profoundly different. I would personally find the politician's job to be equally boring. Susan may find her job to be on the whole more rewarding to her than any other job she could find or prepare for. Of course, almost every job has its dishwashing aspect. I hate to make up tests for my students. There is nothing enjoyable about it; it is certainly not "fulfilling." But the rest of the job is good enough to compensate for my having to make out tests and attend dull committee meetings. Indeed, if we believe the Bible, then we must conclude that not even God takes the same degree of pleasure in every aspect of his divine work. (See Amos 7:3; Jonah 4:2; Exodus 32:12, 14; 1 Samuel 15:35; 2 Samuel 24:16.)

To be sure, there may be good reason why a person should give up one job or work-style in favor of another. But he or she would do well to evaluate a job according to his or her *own* values, interests, talents, opportunities, prior commitments, and many other personal matters. To give up a job simply because someone else labels it as "unfulfilling" is to ignore one's own unique personality. By the same token, to be denied a job because of one's sex, color, or any other irrelevant factor is to be victimized by people whose power over others deserves to be appropriately curtailed. In his book *The Young Evangelicals,* Richard Quebedeaux reminds us that there is nothing especially Christian about ignoring or rationalizing social and economic injustice and prejudice.

Sexual Fulfillment

Despite the increase in the number of books and articles exhorting men and women to be "sexually fulfilled," the surprising fact is that an increasing number of men are reported as sexually impotent. Some psychologists have speculated that the recent failure of some husbands to enjoy even a moderate degree of sexual intercourse with their wives is a result of excessive expectations. Instead of being an enjoyable and supportive experience, sexual intimacy has apparently become for some couples a contest. The playfulness and delight of the experience has been transformed into excessively serious business.

Amid all the talk of sexual fulfillment, we perhaps ought to call a halt long enough to ask ourselves whether anyone knows how much sex is required in order to qualify as "a sexually fulfilling relationship." The Bible nowhere sets forth a general quantitative standard for any and every couple, a standard which each couple can use to determine when sexual fulfillment has been reached. What the Bible does make clear is that sexual intercourse is to be a part of a caring relationship and not simply one of exploitation. The frequency and quantity of sexual climax is not nearly so important as the *quality* of the sexual interaction between husband and wife.

The more or less scientific studies of human sexuality give us no firm conclusion as to how much sexual intercourse a "healthy" marital relationship requires. What can be positively concluded, however, is that some gentle and spontaneous physical stroking each day between husband and wife as well as expressions of physical affection between parents and children do normally carry considerable physical and psychological benefit. Indeed, it is sometimes forgotten that husband and wife do not need to be having intercourse in order to be enjoying each other sexually. Because there are many dimensions of sexuality and because each marriage has intimate and unique qualities of its own to develop, no one can say what sexual fulfillment is for each and every couple. Even when some well-meaning marriage counselors and psychologists advise husband and wife to engage in foreplay, they unconsciously are upholding intercourse as the *ultimate* goal of sexual play, as if every other dimension of sexual enjoyment were a *means* to the climax rather than something of value and meaning for its own sake. Unfortunately, some couples are made to feel that the climax is some goal to *strive* toward and that unless it is attained, the marriage is somehow meaningless and insignificant. Let us hope that this faulty thinking can be exposed and divested of its influence on marriage.

Charismatic Christians

In especially the last five or six years we have been hearing a lot about a group of Christians who are identified with the charismatic movement, which is sometimes called the "tongues movement." Outside the Christian circle is another group claiming to offer us the opportunity to "higher consciousness." In its own way, each of these groups implies at times that if we accept its way of life for ourselves, we will become complete persons, but that if we do not accept it, we will remain at an inferior level of spirituality. I wish to comment on the claims of these two groups.

According to many charismatic Christians, speaking in tongues is both a special gift of the Spirit and an exemplification of higher spirituality. We recall that the Apostle Paul wrote. "I thank God that I speak in tongues more than you all." (1 Cor. 14:18) But instead of requiring tongues for every Christian, Paul went on to add that "nevertheless, in church I would rather speak five words with my mind, in order to instruct others, than ten thousand words in a tongue." (1 Cor 14:19) This is not because speaking publicly from the mind is intrinsically superior to speaking privately in unknown tongues from the heart. Rather, Paul was afraid that outsiders and unbelievers visiting the church might think that the worshiping believers were insane if the believers were heard speaking in unknown tongues. (See 1 Corinthians 14:23.) Paul's recommendation was that, in public, Christians should either speak intelligibly or have an interpreter of everyone who speaks in a tongue that is unknown to the rest of the congregation, including the visistors.

A passage from one of Paul's letters to the Corinthian Christians is appropriate:

> Now you are the body of Christ and individually members of it. And God has appointed in the church first apostles, second prophets, third teachers, then workers of miracles, then healers, helpers, administrators, speakers in various kinds of tongues. (1 Cor. 12:27-28)

Many Christians interpret this to be Paul's way of ranking in order of importance the gifts of the Spirit. Assuming that this is the proper interpretation, we might ask why is one gift more important than another? The answer seems to be that Paul has in mind as his *primary goal* the carrying of the gospel to those who do not believe, so that they may come to believe. Under this goal, being an *apostle* is of first importance because it is through the apostles that the gospel message is revealed. There must be a message before it can be carried. Also, for Paul, an apostle is someone who carries the message. The word "apostle" means "one who is sent forth."

Prophets are the second most important. The function of prophecy, says Paul, is to encourage, upbuild, and bring consolation. (See 1 Corinthians 14:3.) In other words, after people accept the message brought by apostles, then as the church is formed as a body of believers it becomes necessary to support the church by encouragement and upbuilding in general. In addition, a church needs teachers and others to continue the work begun by the apostles.

Paul makes the point that there is a need for a *variety* of gifts. Not all Christians can be apostles or prophets. Not all can speak in tongues. But everyone can *"desire* the higher gifts." (See 1 Corinthians 12:31, italics added.) But what are the higher gifts? If we take the order of gifts as a ranking of importance, then Paul places speaking in tongues at the bottom of the list. Some say that in telling believers to desire the higher gifts, he is not advising everyone to seek to be an apostle or prophet. Indeed, in Paul's thinking, God *calls an apostle* and does not make it a matter of human *desire.* Other Christians say that the higher gifts to be desired are really those coming *after* the office of apostleship. There is some support for this latter interpretation, for Paul does admonish his readers to "earnestly *desire* the spiritual gifts, especially that you may *prophesy."* (1 Cor. 14:1, italics added)

Still other Christians hold that after admonishing the believers to "desire the higher gifts," (1 Cor. 12:31) Paul moves immediately and directly to offer what has become his famous passage on *love*—1 Corinthians 13. Apparently, love is the highest gift—at least according to this interpretation. This interpretation does not conflict with the view of those Christians who hold that prophecy is the highest gift that Christians can *desire.* For when Paul says plainly, "Make love your aim," he tells them to desire especially to prophesy. (1 Cor. 14:1) We have already seen that prophesying includes encouraging, upbuilding, and giving consolation. And that is certainly love in action. Paul, then, makes it quite clear, "He who speaks in a tongue edifies *himself,* but he who prophesies edifies *the church."* (1 Cor. 14:4, italics added) If that is not clear enough, Paul says in addition, "He who prophesies is greater than he who speaks in tongues, unless someone interprets, so that the church may be edified." (1 Cor. 14:5)

Paul wants everyone to speak in tongues, just as he himself speaks in tongues. But he wants them even more to prophesy. (See 1 Corinthians 14:5.) Of course, Paul also wants everyone to remain *single,* just as he himself is single. But he states quite clearly that he knows that not everyone has the special gift of remaining single. (See 1 Corinthians 7:7.) This does not make married people inferior Christians. They simply have a *different* gift. Similarly, if one Christian speaks in a tongue, he or she is not thereby rendered superior to a Christian who does not. He simply has a different gift. Difference in gifts, then, does not necessarily entail superiority in spiritual status.

It is important to understand that, for Paul, no Christian or group of Christians is the whole body of Christ. And if we happen to have the modest gift of humor, perhaps we will see that *not even the whole body of Christ is complete!* The church still lacks a *head* of its own. Christ is the head of the church. Therefore, no member of the body of Christ should even expect to be a completed person. Nevertheless, as an incomplete person, one still has intrinsic value and worth. Perhaps the gift to live joyfully despite human incompleteness is itself a gift available to everyone.

The Proponents of Higher Consciousness

Had we taken seriously every voice challenging us to fulfill ourselves, we would be as leaves tossed about in the wind. It seems as if everywhere we turn there is just one more guru to tell us that we should think of ourselves as crass and low until we throw ourselves into the guru's particular recommended activity or state of mind.

It is one thing to have significant options if we wish to make a significant change in our lives. It is another to be bombarded with gurus, sex sales persons, pushers, or hot shots eager to give us the latest religious "fix." To be sure, there are times when a person's life-style becomes so unrewarding that he or she needs a radical change. Carl Webster, for example, seemed not to be able to make it with the women in the way that he desired. One day, in desperation, he traveled to another country to employ the services of a prostitute. The experience proved to be little more than a fifteen minute business exchange. What frustrated Carl most was the unwillingness of the prostitute to sit and talk with him after their quick physical interchange. Of course, he wanted more than a minimal act of sexual intercourse, but the prostitute had contracted for nothing more. Carl wanted both friendship and sex, but he seemed never to be able to find them together.

Becoming increasingly disgusted with his life, Al eventually found himself involved in a new exotic religion. Today he is immersed in this religion, so much so that he stands eager to convert everyone he possibly can. It appears to anger him that people will not accept what he thinks is the absolute truth and perfect way of life. In many ways, he may be compared to a Don Juan who cannot be happy until he has seduced all the prospects that his energy will permit.

Today he regards himself as having gone through a profound change. Time will tell whether his journeys into the exotic religion have, in fact, tempered his inordinate lust for power over others. In any case, he claims that a person who has not experienced the "higher consciousness" that he offers must remain spiritually inferior because he or she lacks the highest degree of truth, knowledge, insight, love, etc. Al enjoys telling many people whom he meets that he has something that they lack, something which, by implication, renders them spiritually inferior to himself. He will give free and absolute advice on how to be rid of headaches and will even calculate for some people the year when they will die. He thinks of himself as divine, which is certainly a rise in status and self-importance.

Kundalini Yoga, with its reputed journey through seven stages, claims to lead us into a consciousness beyond even the medieval Christian mystics, who promised the beatific vision. It is not difficult to come upon people each day who are eager to instruct us in "higher consciousness." Some hold to three stages of consciousness, others to more stages. Usually, we are told that the East is where our salvation lies. The West is said to be too mundane for anything spiritual and elevated.

I suggest that perhaps what some people call "higher consciousness" is a *different* consciousness; it is an experience that is different from other experiences. But something's being different does not necessarily entail that it is "higher" or superior in any universal sense. Indeed, it may well be that what is a rewarding experience for some people is relatively unrewarding for others. Of course, mystics cannot imagine someone having a mystical experience and then finding something else that is more or equally rewarding. But this possibility should not be ruled out arbitrarily.

The remarkable composer J. S. Bach was not from the mysterious East but from Germany. As far as I know, the East has never produced music like Bach's. Is the East therefore inferior? The East is definitely musically inferior to the West *if* music of the quality of Bach's is used as the standard. We can imagine a lively discussion between a guru from the East and a fan of Bach, a discussion in which each locates the other far down the ladder of spiritual experience or awareness. I myself enjoy hiking in the mountains and stopping along the way to feel the ferns and listen to the wind "OM" through the trees, or simply looking up the side of a tree to watch the clouds mingle with the autumn leaves. To some people, this experience is "ho hum." To me, it is joyous beyond description. Without doubt, there have been many people who have visited the California and Arizona deserts only to come away with no deep appreciation of the tiny flowers, the desert silence, the infinite variety of rock formations, the surprises of the desert night. I am equally sure that there are many dimensions of life to which we all remain oblivious. Hence, for anyone to claim that he or she has the *ultimate* experience—in some super ontological sense—is indeed to make a claim. But other people make equally strong claims about quite *different* experiences.

The hard fact is that people often differ profoundly as to what kind of experience is most meaningful to them. It is not surprising that when individuals find something profoundly meaningful to them, they cannot help believing that all others will find it equally meaningful in the same way if only they will open their hearts and minds.

Perhaps there is no one sort of experience that is most meaningful for everyone. Perhaps there is no universal higher consciousness. Why should we demand that there be? Consider the difficulty—perhaps the impossibility—of giving a universal and permanent answer to such questions as the following: "For the truly fulfilled person, is a plum tree in the autumn more beautiful than the mystical experience is enlightening?" "Is hearing Mozart's

'Sonata III' more 'ultimate' than uttering 'OM'?'' "Is meditation more genuine than the love of a husband for his wife?'' "Is the sexual experience more enriching than a walk in a spring rain?'' "Is the flower in the crannied wall more profound to contemplate than is what some gurus call the seventh stage of awareness?'' "Is mystical 'insight' more meaningful than the mother's caring love of her child?'' "Can any substitute be found for the love between father and son, or between brother and brother?''

Mystics claim deep insight. But perhaps there is an insight—or option—to equal the mystics', namely, the insight that even ordinary things are extraordinary. Aspects of general revelation may be seen in a new light, or felt as never felt before, or experienced as never experienced before. Suppose we ask, "What is true 'higher consciousness'?'' That is a bit like asking how silent is silence? Or, how beautiful is beauty? It is not surprising that we have conflicting answers about what is "higher consciousness.''

Living with Incompleteness

We may count ourselves fortunate indeed that our human enjoyment and meaningfulness does not require of us a completeness of being. Jesus may have actually used humor to expose the myth of human completeness. Some Christians seem to think that Jesus never laughed, but it may be that he had a very delightful sense of humor. If so, then perhaps light can be thrown on his statement "Be ye therefore perfect, even as your Father which is in heaven is perfect.'' (Matt. 5:48 K.J.V.) While we cannot be sure of what the original context for this statement was, we may venture to say that Jesus was using humor to deal with some of the self-righteous Pharisees. He may have said in effect: If you insist on talking of your superiority over others, then why do you not measure yourselves up to *the real standard of completeness and perfection.* Be as perfect as your Father in heaven!

Needless to say, the absurdity of the comparison between God and people should have startled some of the Pharisees sufficiently to make them see that they had no genuine basis for thinking themselves to be morally complete and perfect. The conspicuous truth is that no human being measures up to the highest ideal of personhood, parenthood, spousehood, brotherhood, or sisterhood. But that does not mean that all our efforts and human relationships are therefore worthless. To be sure, they do not count as merits toward purchasing salvation, but they do have intrinsic worth and meaning at the human level, which is what, for most Christians, the doctrine of divine grace entails.

Historians often charge that Christianity in the Middle Ages looked upon earthly life as hardly more than a proving ground where each person tests oneself in order to prove worthy of the next life. Whether or not this is an accurate description of Christians at that time, it certainly is not true of Christianity today. Turning the present life into a *means only* is foreign to belief in divine grace. In grace, people may live enjoyably and meaningfully despite their incompleteness. They are not required to prove themselves absolutely worthy of enjoying life. Earthly existence is not simply a stepping stone, but is intrinsically meaningful and worthwhile. A thirty-year-old man once complained to me, "It seems as if I've been spending all my life just *getting ready* to live." It is not surprising, therefore, that he had been thinking seriously of his own suicide.

One of the great ironies of history is that the so-called Protestant Work Ethic developed without taking seriously the famous Protestant emphasis on grace and "justification by faith." This irony is so influential in our practical lives today that it will be quite enlightening to look further into it.

Ascetic Protestantism

One of the most provocative studies of Christian life is Max Weber's *The Protestant Ethic and the Spirit of Capitalism,*[5] which is a study of relationships between Protestantism and the economic and social life in modern Western culture. Weber shows how what he calls "ascetic Protestantism" has turned all of our economic existence into a kind of monastic and ascetic activity. I am not concerned here to plunge into the important scholarly debates as to whether Weber's thesis is warranted at every point or whether his treatment of "ascetic Protestantism" can be applied to Protestantism in general. All I will say is that I do *not* believe that "ascetic Protestantism" is a logical outcome of legitimate Protestant belief. Nevertheless, a lot of people in Protestant churches (and now in Catholic churches, too) have adopted for themselves a version of this so-called ascetic Protestantism, which is, to use Weber's phrase, "an iron cage."

Very briefly, Weber's position is as follows. For various reasons (which can be ignored here) some branches of Protestant Christianity came to look upon the entire world as something of a vast monastery. In this cloister, each Christian believer is to think of himself as a monk, busy depriving himself of the ordinary joys and pleasures of life so that he could devote all his energies in the service of his duties in the worldly monastery of business activity. According to this thesis, unlike the Roman Catholic monk, the Protestant monk (which is supposed to be every Protestant) is called upon to take a spouse only as a service and duty to God. (Imagine: kissing your spouse because it is a *duty!*) The purpose of marriage for ascetic Protestants is simple: to produce children and to raise them to become themselves ascetic Protestant priests or monks in the monastery of the world. The ascetic seventeenth century preacher Richard Baxter went so far as to desire to strip Christian living of close human friendship, as if the world were some sort of busy factory and God were the foreman who strictly prohibits any fraternizing on the job. And, of course, for ascetic Protestantism, the Christian is always supposed to be on the job and infected with the "work mentality."

It is important to understand just how radical this branch of Protestantism really is. Most people had thought of the monastery as having a very routinized, highly structured, and very rigorous program. There was little place for the spontaneous delights of the easy-going interchange of social life that existed outside the monastery. The monastery was, above all, very serious and somber business. It was certainly not expected that every Christian would fit into this style of life. Most would be unable to do so. The monk's or nun's life was regarded by many Catholics as

the supreme human achievement on earth. But while they admired
it, most Christians did not *envy* it.

Ascetic Protestantism, however, changed all this. The monk-
ish life of hard, serious, rigorous discipline void of the gaiety and
enrichments of life outside the monastery was expected to be the
envy of *every* true Christian. Indeed, especially the world of *work*
was to be regarded as the divine "calling" of every true Christian.
Just as monks spent long hours praying, confessing their sins and
attending to other strictly "religious" duties, so the new ascetic
Protestants were to engage zealously in economic production and
profit-making as if such were a holy "calling."

Of course, Christianity of both Catholic and Protestant forms
has emphasized that the believer is to work honestly at a job.
But the new professional asceticism turned practically everything
into work. Play itself became suspect. If there was to be play, it
must be regarded as something to *work* at, perhaps even something on which to make a profit. Some of the old Calvinists used
to say that the purpose of a human life was to both serve God
and enjoy him forever. But the ascetic Protestants seemed to forget the second part—to *enjoy* God. I suspect that the contemporary emphasis upon "fulfillment" has more of the old ascetic
"work ethic" than we like to believe. The call to fulfill oneself
has become a kind of religious duty—or, to be more accurate, a
kind of neurotic compulsion. In its more perverted form, a fulfilling life is interpreted to be a "calling" to *fill one's life full*—so
full that there is no time for ordinary enjoyment, delight, appreciation, or even self-acceptance. I have for years been struck by
the obsession that some ascetics seem to have to "improve themselves." Paradoxically, they are so terribly busy improving themselves that they seldom have time to take *pleasure* in what they
have done. They seem always to be "getting ready" to live, making preparations, but never experiencing much joy in the process.

To be sure, it would be quite foolish to ignore the hard
fact that much of our life cannot be enjoyed unless we do plan
ahead, postpone some of our gratifications, and defer certain enjoyments. What I am saying, however, is that some life-styles

locate practically every major enjoyment in the *future,* so that the present, robbed of its reality, becomes a kind of shadow of what is promised for the future. The future with its promises seems never to turn into the present with its fundamental enjoyments. What is lacking in such a life-style is a certain grace in living— religious grace in the sense of accepting the present as not only an opportunity to prepare well for future enjoyments, but as an opportunity to delight in the daily blessings that fall across our paths. Indeed, I doubt that we will be able to plan intelligently for future enjoyments until in the *present* we experience gentle delight, joy, and pleasure.

To plan for the future, even if it means sometimes sacrificing a measure of present happiness, is a *practical* necessity. But it need not become a *neurotic* necessity. That is, people need not sacrifice most of the process of living in order to appease some idolatrous image of themselves as The Completed Being. The Christian believes that under divine grace he or she has an imputed *right* to a realistic chance at earthly happiness and enjoyment, even though life is perpetually incomplete and unfulfilled in many ways.

My daughter once told me that she wished she were fifteen instead of eight. I sat down then and there and explained that after a few months she would never never again be eight years old. "I can't ever be eight again, nor can your mother," I continued. Then my daughter added that her brother could not be eight again. I went on to say that being eight is something very special and that in time she could be another age and could enjoy living a whole year at that age, too. She got the point and elaborated on it herself. Not since then has she expressed a desire to be another age. The sum and substance of this chapter is that each age—and each day—usually has some value, intrinsic to itself, that is completely irreplaceable by any other age or day. In realizing that this is the case, perhaps we can place to the side the myth of completeness in order to enjoy our diverse styles of incompleteness under grace.

Dr. Wayne Oates, one of my psychology professors of many years ago, once stated in class that "Hard work never hurt anybody!" But about ten or so years after that, Dr. Oates was forced to give up some of his work in order not to lose his health permanently. A few years later he wrote a very practical and revealing little book entitled *Confessions of a Workaholic,*[6] which serves as a wise and humorous commentary on his earlier declaration that hard work never hurt anyone.

I do not wish to be interpreted as advocating mediocrity in our work. Far from it. Rather I am saying something very simple, namely, that there are only a relatively few things that we can do expertly. Most avenues in life we will not even venture into because of limits of time and other factors. Hence, when we see how very finite and limited we are, then perhaps we will not be so upset if someone labels us as incomplete. We might even smile and agree. And instead of fretting over our incompleteness, we can be thankful that we had the chance to be born at all.

When Young Christians Look for Work

This year, when many young Christians go out to find jobs, they will learn that if they are women, they will[7] on the whole find very few interesting jobs. And they will also find the pay to be less than what men of their own age and training enjoy. Many poorly paid female secretaries are already better educated than their male bosses. I am not here asking the Christian churches to work actively for fair treatment of women and other minorities on the job market. With some noble exceptions, many Christian churches have been quite reluctant to be leaders in working for "fair treatment" of any group. All I ask for here is that these churches not get in the way of those who are concerned to see improvement in better working conditions for people everywhere.

Perhaps it is because most Christians are sensitive to the special revelation of the Bible that they seem so insensitive to the hardships of people in their jobs and vocations. Perhaps it is because they are concerned to prepare people for the next life that they seem so unconcerned that great throngs of people in this life are finding their jobs to be meaningless and repressive. But Christinaity as a *view of life* is more sensitive and open than often indicated by its adherents. And within this view of life there is room for belief that God can use pagans and others to accomplish his purposes on earth. According to Isaiah 45, Yahweh God selected the pagan King Cyrus as his "anointed one" to carry out divine purposes. It is open, therefore, for Christians to believe that God may today use pagan economists, sociologists, psychologists, and other behavioral scientists to help do something constructive about the depressing working situations of many people in various nations. With their ear to general revelation, behavioral scientists may come forth with options and alternatives which Christians themselves might never bring forth. I personally doubt that Marxism will offer very much in terms of creative practical alternatives, although I see no reason why Christians should not learn something from even Marxist economists if they happened to develop some useful options. In this connection, they will wish to keep in mind what Paul said about God's turning to the Gentiles in order "to make Israel jealous." (Rom. 11:11)

Many Christians seem genuinely and rightly worried that the youthful followers of the Reverend Moon are increasing in number. We complain about the way he exploits young people and works them while offering very little economic rewards to the youthful workers. Moon himself is fabulously rich, to a great extent because he has so many dedicated workers who pull in large sums of money for him each week. However, people are inconsistent when they denounce Moon but say nothing about other business exploiters who, while working young and old alike, often pay indecent wages and provide jobs that kill the spirit and turn creative humans into functioning work-animals for forty hours a week.

We might respect at least the *consistency* of those Christians who do not even promise that their faith will make life on this earth more interesting and rewarding in itself. But what can be said of those Christians who *do promise* a more rewarding life on earth but who endeavor to do nothing about making life at the factory, shop, or office more interesting and enjoyable? We must ask this one question: "Are some Christians saying by their actions that earthly life can be rewarding only *after* an individual

gets off from work each day?'' If that is what they are saying,
then it is only sensible to hope that they will at least keep to
the side and out of the way of those who are sincerely engaging
in ways of improving earthly human working conditions. There
are no biblical grounds for telling people to work hard and faithfully *regardless of working conditions and level of income.* But this
fact will not prevent some from turning any kind of work into a
fetish and then sanctioning it as if it were an unconditional divine
calling.

I admit that some of my Christian friends may not respond
favorably to the suggestion that to a large extent they have confused their biblical faith with certain dehumanizing economic and
social practices. Whether this confusion can be cleared up in the
near future remains to be seen. Let me conclude by admitting that
I do not know what can be done on a large scale to improve the
quality and conditons of work in our society. But there is *no theological and religious reason* why evangelical Christians cannot be
actually engaged in seeking to improve the conditions.

> In reality, there are precious few jobs that make much use
> of higher-order skills, training, or intelligence. The Bureau
> of Labor Statistics estimates that only about 20 percent
> of all jobs will require a college education for successful
> performance in 1980. More depressing, the Office of Man-
> agement and Budget finds that one half of all current jobs
> do not even require a high school education.

A minimal hope is that if Christians decline to contribute constructively to the goal of improving the quality of work, they will
at least think it possible that God might be bringing forth a merciful result of economic and social reform without their aid.

Because the Jehovah's Witnesses regard politics to be nothing but the manifestation of original sin, they do not vote or participate in political processes. If Christians think that they have
no contribution to make in economic and work reforms, then
perhaps they will at least not work against those who do try to
make a positive contribution. It was a disturbing thought to some

of the Hebrew people to learn from Isaiah that God could use a pagan as his "anointed one." Christians must not be surprised if they discover the elevating work of God to be carried on by agents other than Christians themselves.

It ought to be said that Christians can still make a profound contribution even when they are not themselves the creative thrust of economic and social reform. They can serve in a negative way and a positive way (1) by exposing the aspects of movements that are tyrannical and repressive and (2) by supporting reforms that would seem to help eliminate greater misery than they create. This two-fold contribution should not be underrated; for it entails having an open mind and heart, a willingness to listen to the alternatives, and a sensitivity to what the problems are that cause so much human suffering and psychological depletion. In this book I have tried to say that there are various sources in the world that can be selectively called upon to help strengthen the institution of marriage and the family. But there is also the responsibility that the family has to the wider community. If one spouse chooses to work for a particular social "cause," the other may help indirectly by encouraging him or her in the cause. There are many different ways to support a cause.

In supporting causes, a couple would be wise to recognize early that each of them can give only so much time and money. They should not feel guilty because they are not infinite or do not have unlimited resources. The family conference is the place to discuss commitments to causes and to pledge support for each other in the pursuit of these causes. Anthony and Marilyn Deats are on the verge of a divorce, despite the fact that they have six children. One of the children stole an automobile, another has been in serious trouble, and so on. Marilyn in particular has been very faithful in taking the children to church, and the Deats are very decent, considerate, concerned human beings. We cannot, therefore, help asking, "What happened?"

A careful look at the family reveals that Anthony is a very committed and dedicated man. He is a very concerned man. But he could not say, "No, thank you; I am a limited, finite human being." When his church asked him not to limit his family size by using artificial birth control methods, he could not say no to his church. When concerned citizens asked him to serve on a very important committee, he could not say no because of his profound concern. Nor could he resist the many requests to run for office in his town. In short, Anthony was a very concerned and socially alert person. But he was also a limited human being who had failed to see how very limited his time and energy were.

In effect, he did, without realizing it, say no to his own children, and the price he has paid for this has been enormous. So, with good and kind motives, but with limited self-understanding, Anthony Deats has sacrificed much of his family.

I would be among the last to depreciate the very outstanding things that this man has done for his community. Unfortunately, the community did not return the favor so freely by helping Anthony and Marilyn to hold their family together. Perhaps in a day of important social causes, we who are married should remind ourselves that *marriage and the family are themselves worthy social causes.* In realizing this, we might devote ourselves more enjoyably and eagerly to the challenge of raising our children and growing together with our spouse.

IX

DEALING
WITH THE
UNEXPECTED

With Children You Can Count on the Unexpected

Have you ever known parents whose kids turned out exactly as the parents expected them to turn out? I have counseled with a number of young people who were made to feel guilty because they had failed to become interested in pursuing the line of work recommended by their father or mother. Sometimes parents make themselves miserable by forgetting that they simply cannot have complete control of their offspring. It is wise to try to prepare one's child for a variety of jobs and thereby increase the child's options at the time when he or she must go to work. But to insist on one career for one's offspring is usually in our culture nothing short of tyranny.

Most of us are not very sympathetic with those parents who are frustrated because their son or daughter declines to follow the parents' choice of careers. We more easily sympathize with parents whose children grow up to reject the values and religious faith of their parents. In the Bible, one of the most heart-breaking stories is that of the destroyed relationship between David and his son Absalom. Those of us who complain too readily about our children might profit by reading the account of Absalom's conspiracy to overthrow his own father in battle and to become king in his place. Not only that, "Absalom went in to his father's concubines in the sight of all Israel." (2 Sam. 16:22 R.S.V.)

Still David could not bring himself to hate his own son. Forced eventually to prepare to stand to defend his people against the army of Absalom, David made one final request of Joab, David's chief military officer. As Joab was leaving with the army, David was overheard saying to Joab. " 'Deal gently for my sake with the young man Absalom.' " (2 Sam. 18:5 R.S.V.) We all know David's reaction upon learning that his son had been killed in battle.

> *And the king was deeply moved, and went up to the chamber over the gate, and wept; and as he went, he said, "O my son Absalom, my son, my son Absalom! Would I had died instead of you. O Absalom, my son, my son!" (2 Sam. 18:33)*

Looking back over David's past life, we can find a number of mistakes and transgressions that he committed. But we still find ourselves moved by this father's tragedy, for to have one's own son turn against oneself is an excruciating emotional death. In a strange sort of way the account of Absalom may bring comfort to us who are parents, for when compared to David, most of us appear not to have lost in the hopeless way that David lost. Twenty-five years ago a devout Christian worried for a long time over the fact that her son seemed not to be interested in becoming a minister. The young man was not a rebellious son; he simply did not think he should be a minister. Today he is a deacon in a Baptist church and a dean at a Baptist college. The mother really has no basis for complaint and simply worried herself unnecessarily.

Other parents, however, earn our genuine compassion, for they have watched their sons and daughters either become criminals or suffer serious injuries and tragedies in their lives. It is true that regarding our children, we tend to lose perspective. Recently a young woman in her early twenties told me that it had become difficult for her to talk to her father, who was the pastor of a nearby church. In the course of a conversation, she revealed that they could not talk with each other because she had changed some of her theological views and did not agree with some of what her father had been preaching all his adult life. Very often parents forget that a disagreement between parents and offspring on some issues—as important as they are—does not necessarily mean that the offspring have given up *every* moral and religious value and belief that they received at home. I encouraged the young woman to sit down with her father and to write down together some of the basic values and beliefs which the two of them still shared. It often amazes parents and offspring alike to discover how many beliefs and values they still share despite some very profound differences.

Richard, a boy of twelve, and his father have worked out a deal with one another. When the father is correcting Richard exceedingly and is making it seem that the boy does nothing right, Richard is supposed to say simply, "Don't forget the 99 percent, Dad." This brief statement is designed to remind the father of what both he and his son want the father to remember, namely, that over 99 percent of the time Richard's behavior and attitudes are very responsible. This short reminder helps the father to set his criticism in perspective and, in addition, to encourage the son to continue to be a responsible person.

If you have children of nine years of age or older, you might find it very rewarding to take the time to review in your mind how many destructive and cruel things they *could* do but *do not* in fact do. For example, Bill Harper's son is strong enough to kick a hole in the living room walls or choke his sister when he is angry. He is intelligent and skilled enough to design traps that could mutilate all the neighborhood cats. Bill's daughter is able to phone the neighbors and use abusive language, or even slash the tires of her teacher's car. There are literally thousands upon thousands of destructive and cruel options which Bill's children might do but do not. When he thinks about this, his own anger and anxiety seems to cool down and his appreciation for his children rises remarkably. They are not perfect kids; but, then, neither is Bill a perfect parent.

If Your Son or Daughter Loses Interest in Church

Now, it often happens that when young people reach about the age of 15 or so, they resist going to church and Sunday School. This is frequently a very disturbing experience to parents who have tried to raise their children in the faith. Sometimes youths are only testing to determine whether their parents really do care about the religious life of their offspring. Unfortunately, it is not always possible to know in advance whether the son or daughter is testing or whether the church experience has in fact lost its meaning and significance to the youth. So it takes a bit of ingenuity to know what to do in this upsetting period.

There is one rule, however, that should normally be followed. After a youth becomes fifteen years old, it is very doubtful that *forcing* one to go to church will do more good than harm. But there are other options. The first option is to become a very receptive and non-punishing audience for your child to speak to. This may eventually encourage a young person to talk. After all, there may be some legitimate complaint about the church. The next step is to suggest possible avenues for an individual to follow that will allow for church experience without having to endure some of the aspects that may be meaningless or exceedingly frustrating. It may very well be that a teen-ager will visit or join another church in the city in which you live. True, it may be an inconvenience for you, but you may be glad to endure it in order to strengthen your offspring's efforts in looking for a meaningful church experience.

Perhaps there is an interesting boy or girl from another family who is going to another church. It would be short-sighted of any parents to oppose strongly their child's desire to go to that other church. Indeed, the parents should rejoice that their offspring not only will be going to church but will be interested in young people who are also going to church. As a youth, I once heard some adults in the church complain that the teen-agers came to church to court. The minister of the church was quick to demonstrate common sense realism when he commented, "What better place for young people to court than at the church!"

In dealing with the offspring's loss of interest in church, parents would do well to ask whether their offspring's lack of interest is in religion or simply in a particular local church. In writing this section of the chapter I asked my son to come to my study to give me some help on this topic. He suggested that young people might become more interested in church if certain changes within the local church itself were made to meet some of the needs of the young people. For example, he recommended new youth groups with new goals, or a new relationship with the minister, or new projects and programs. I know one minister who thinks it worthwhile to have a group of children in his church called "Pastor's Pals." He takes them swimming and to other outings on a regular basis so that they will have a Christian adult to relate to and to enjoy under wholesome conditions.

What my son's suggestions add up to is some willingness on the part of influential adults of the church to make adjustments and reforms that will meet the youths' needs religiously and even socially. If we want our young people to feel that their home church is really their home church, then they must have some voice in its program. There is no biblical basis for assuming that the Spirit of God moves in the hearts of only those who are over nineteen years old.

Of course, it may be that regardless of what changes are made to interest our offspring in staying in the church, they may still choose not to go. It is important, especially at this very crucial and emotional time, that threats not be utilized. It is a time when parents and others in the church must do all they can to *encourage one another* to remain calm and to practice creative listening. By listening to their teen-ager, parents may be surprised to learn that he or she is not rejecting Christianity, but rather is seeking some independence of mind and heart—which, incidentally, is what many Baptists, Presbyterians, and others once fought for and won.

If the son or daughter still chooses not to go to church, then perhaps in the course of calm conversation and exploration, the parent and offspring may come up with still another option. Instead of going to Sunday School, the son or daughter may be open to the alternative of reading books on Christian living or on biblical studies and Christian doctrine. Indeed, it may very well be that in this way he or she will learn far more about Christianity than he or she would in the average slow-moving Sunday School class. Perhaps the son or daughter could be encouraged to bring some of his or her questions and observations to the minister or to someone else at the church who is deemed trustworthy and receptive.

The point here is that there exist all kinds of resources available to help keep young people interested in the Christian faith. Instead of insisting that the son or daughter develop his or her religious life in exactly the way that they do, parents would do well to search out other acceptable options and to encourage—without threatening—their son or daughter to select Christian options that are most meaningful to him or her at his or her particular stage in life. After all, all true Christians are pilgrims. No one has reached on earth the final stage of Christian growth.

The Appeal of the Cults and the Erotic

Many Christian parents are worried that their children will be led astray into one of the many "cults" that are emerging today. J. Marse Grant, editor of the Baptist publication *The Biblical Recorder*, expressed this concern as follows:

> There is too much evidence that the various cults and
> sects are very efficient at proselytising; that is,
> reaching out to bring in those who are already members
> of the more traditional churches. The message to Baptists
> ought to be clear. If you doubt the seriousness of
> this trend, talk to a parent who has lost a youngster
> to one of the aggressive cults. It'll break your heart.[1]

There is no need here to go into detail regarding what these cults teach and practice. I have in mind the Children of God, the Mormons, the Jehovah's Witnesses, and the various cults of India that come into the United States by way of Los

Angeles, Dallas, Philadelphia, Denver, and other metropolitan areas. Church leaders are justly disturbed that these cults and many others are deliberately attempting to influence youths to forsake their faith. The threat of the cults is increasing and is quite serious.

But what can be done to combat this threat? I doubt that there is any one thing to be done. But several courses of action are open, some of which I will go into now. First, why not express these parental anxieties to the young people of the church. Why not use this anxiety about the cults as an occasion to "open up" communication between adults and young people, to cross over the generation gap.

Second, in meeting with the young people on this matter, parents can learn what some of their children's school friends think of the cults. What do the cults provide religiously, psychologically, and in other ways? Third, out of this coming together some genuinely new and appealing programs in the church could be formulated for examining some of the cults and for comparing them to one's own Christian faith. It is important that sarcasm and ridicule not be employed to put down any cult. People must have confidence in their own faith, so much so that they will not be hesitant to let the light of Scripture direct the course of the comparative study. Indeed, one of the best ways to encourage some young people to become interested in the study of the Bible is to begin with the appeal of the cults, many of which claim to be based on the Bible in some sense. This claim can be examined. The young people of the church can bring their Bibles and together with the adults of the church, search the Scriptures for themselves. In fact, this way of studying the Bible may be quite meaningful because it is done with some definite purpose in mind.

The fourth point that I wish to make on this subject is that the church is not the building. The church is the believers themselves. It may be that the youths would like to meet in the homes of some of the adults. There is no reason why Bible study cannot be combined with a party at someone's home. Young people are much more flexible than some of us imagine.

Because parents are not infallible and because parents do not and cannot control every cue and stimulus that goes into their children, they cannot be certain that their child will not be unduly influenced by one of the many cults. Parents cannot be absolutely certain that their child will not become heavily involved with drugs or alcohol. Nevertheless, many parents do have at least a good fighting chance. Things are not so bad as to force parents to conclude that all their efforts are to no avail.

But wisdom is needed if our efforts are not to be wasted on hopeless or grandiose schemes. This month a mother from another city phoned in order to persuade me to work actively to help enact more laws against pornography. After talking with her a number of times, I had to conclude that the woman was very active but ineffective. I could not justify taking time away from my wife and children in order to join her misconceived campaign. Unfortunately, her crusade had not even made clear what exactly the enemy was and how it could be defeated. There are lots of things that I wish to protect my children from. Violence and depersonalized sexuality are two of them. But there are some things that parents are going to have to do themselves, without the aid of special state or federal laws. In my judgment, the mother who phoned me, while concerned to save my kids and every other child from disaster, was in effect neglecting her own children.

What I am suggesting is that parents have only so much time and energy. It is therefore imperative to see that by shooting for impossible goals, they fail to devote themselves to areas in which they can be reasonably effective. There has never been a Christian nation on earth and never will be. But there have been many Christian homes and families. It would seem, therefore, that parents would do well to cultivate their children in the faith or win their friends and neighbors to Christ, rather than spend their energy in attempting to use the government to *force* unbelievers to give up looking at the "girlie" magazines or reading "cheap" novels.

Christians who think that they can turn an earthly nation into a Christian nation are neither realists nor biblical in their outlook. As one spokesman notes, some sincere Christians dream of "utopian conditions that overlook the limits that original sin places on history."[2] To attempt to utilize political power to eliminate all pornography from the face of the earth, or even from your home town, or mine, is to be distracted from the more fundamental Christian vocation. I myself think that something should be done to make TV a more acceptable medium. Regarding this, the editor of the *Baptist and Reflector* makes a very good point: "If people want to see a wife-swapping movie, let them go to a theatre and pay their money."[3]

Unfortunately, the issue of censorship is very complicated. Even the Baptist editor quoted above seems to think that most Americans are in agreement with evangelical values and that therefore TV ought to reflect only those values. I doubt that this assumption can be supported. Indeed, I would like to pose this question: On what biblical grounds are we to assume that TV ought to be an exclusively Christian medium? Also I wish to ask why it is that so many people seem to oppose strongly violence and sex on TV but have altogether *closed their eyes to the evil of covetousness which is clearly promoted by TV commercials.* As one who regards coveting to be a very great evil, I am strongly opposed to having my children exposed constantly to propaganda which on TV is misleadingly called "advertisement" and "a commercial message."

A realistic proposal dealing with undesirable programs might be for Christians to publish in advance their own evaluations of TV programs. In that way, Christian parents could choose not to have undesirable programs piped into their homes via TV, just as they already choose not to view movies of which they disapprove. I would add also that, in order to reduce the infringement on our precious time and our senses, all TV commercials should be shown at only specially designated times, if at all, in a day or evening. Hence, those who *choose* to watch them may do so by freely dialing a *program of TV commercials.* The TV companies' practice of inserting commercials into those programs that we *choose* to watch is a cynical infringement on our choice. Many of us would strongly protest if, in the middle of one of our chosen TV programs, some wholly irrelevant scene of violence and sexual perversity were injected. By the same token, I am protesting strongly against the practice of injecting *commercials* into my chosen TV programs and those of my children, for the commercials are not simply desired information but are unsolicited stimulants designed to arouse our desires and passions. In short, they generate the sin of covetousness.

Most commercials not only encourage covetousness but exemplify lying or bearing false witness. Some Christians seem to think that the prevention of adultery is the only point of the Ten Commandments. They play down "Thou shalt not covet" and "Thou shalt not bear false witness." If people *want* to receive, via TV, stimuli leading to covetousness, or *want* to be bombarded with violence and perverted sex or *want* to be lied to, then let them have it. But there are others of us who want just as strongly to have some better options. Some parents— myself included—are willing to pay money for the kind of TV programs that we prefer. (Paid TV!) However, there seem to be still too many Christians who are not willing to put their money where their values are.

America and Europe went through a stage when one Christian denomination attempted to impose its faith on the whole country and to throw political weight in support of some Established Religion. Fortunately, the principle of voluntarism prevailed so that today neither your faith nor your neighbor's altogether different faith is outlawed. Today Christians are facing the crisis of whether they are going to try by political power to impose on their fellow citizens an *Established Morality*. I think that this utopian venture will fail also. But just as evangelical Christianity has thrived amid the plurality of faiths, so will its morality continue to thrive amid the plurality of other life-styles. This does not mean that each group can morally approve of the other's faith or life-style, but it does mean that each can live with this diversity, within certain limits, at least. We must not forget that once Christians were persecuted by the Roman Empire because Christians were widely thought to be the corrupters of morality. In the first half of the seventeenth century, Presbyterians would likely have set themselves up as the state church of England had not other Christians prevented this from coming about.[4]

The point here is that Christianity has room for considerable religious disagreement and it is unlikely that a politically enforced Establishment of Christian Morality could be agreed upon as quickly as some Christians seem to think.

The Case of the Questionable Magazine

Brad Noble caught his teen-age son, Jimmy, looking at a copy of *Playboy*, which Jimmy had brought home with him. To be sure, Brad had not expected Jimmy to do this and was somewhat surprised. But instead of condemning his son to hell, Brad told him that he could keep the magazine if he wanted to so long as it was kept out of public sight. (Brad was no fool; he knew full well that if Jimmy really wanted to view the pictures in the magazine, he could do so at the drug store and without either the knowledge or permission of his parents.) Brad then sat down with his son and very gently began to explain that women were persons and not things or objects. The father was very thankful that he was able to recall Paul's advice: "Fathers, do not provoke your children, lest they become discouraged." (Col. 3:21 R.S.V.)

It will prove useful to inquire further into this case in order to see how the concerned father handled this unexpected turn in his son's life. Brad was able to keep his presence of mind sufficiently to be able to realize what he did and did not want to happen in the situation. First, he did not want to humiliate his son or to extract from him a tearful confession that he was a worthless pervert. Second, he did not want to read into Jimmy's action more than what was in fact there. Third, and more positively, what Brad wanted most of all was to take this as an occasion to plant the seed for the development of a healthy attitude toward sex in his son's mind. So, this is all that the father did upon that unexpected occasion—he planted a few seeds of thought in his son's mind and heart.

Now, as every farmer knows, seeds do not take root immediately and do not grow into trees overnight. Brad was able to recognize that he could do only a bit upon the occasion of discovering the *Playboy* magazine in his son's possession. But at later times, and under less pressured conditions, Brad was able to cultivate and nurture the thoughts that he had earlier left with his son.

Any good gardner or farmer knows that usually before seeds are planted, the ground must be tilled or plowed. Fortunately, Brad had already over the years tilled the ground. That is, he had over the years built up a respectful but stable relationship with his son, which meant that the unexpected incident of his son's looking at the magazine was not something to be taken out of perspective. The incident was more like new weeds in the garden, weeds that could gradually be controlled, rather than a sudden and fierce attack of devastating locusts.

Many Christians are sometimes more prone than they have a right to be to see changes in children as *nothing but* unmixed expressions of original sin. When serving as the president of the Fuller Theological Seminary, the late Dr. E.J. Carnell noted that to be under the curse of original sin "does not mean that we are as bad as we might be ...."[5] Rather it means that every aspect of human life is touched by sin, which, however, is different from saying that each aspect is as corrupt and rotten as it could possibly be.

The point here is that Jimmy's looking at the pictures in *Playboy* was not a one hundred percent evil act. It was doubtless mixed with the wholesome element of curiosity and sensitivity to novelty. It takes a wise father to be able to appreciate curiosity while at the same time correcting any unhealthy views of sex that his son might have.

On a later occasion, Brad talked with his son about one of the major disadvantages of having pictures of nude females in his room. He also talked about an immoral aspect of the pictures. As Harvey Cox and other Christian writers have noted, the *Playboy* philosophy tends to regard women as objects or things. Brad explained to Jimmy that girls and women are persons, not impersonal objects. The practice of looking at nude females could easily encourage Jimmy to think of females in depersonalized terms, viewing them as mere instruments of his own pleasure and not as human persons of intrinsic value and worth.

Pictures of nude young women could also have a personal disadvantage for Jimmy. Bradley pointed out to him that in some sense sexual arousal is like hunger for food. With little difficulty Jimmy could understand that it would be a mistake for a person on a diet to place pictures of delicious food in his or her room. A picture of either a rich pecan pie or an enticing plate of hot cakes, butter, and syrup would set in motion certain points and parts of the dieter's body. This, in turn, would make it more difficult for the dieter to resist the body's moving toward the kitchen or to the market to get the food to eat. To control the body's tendency to be drawn to food, the dieter would be foolish indeed to leer at enticing pictures of barbequed pork or fried shrimp. By the same token, Bradley explained, Jimmy would be foolish to keep pictures of nude girls in his room, for they might stimulate sexual arousal.

In the course of conversation, the father and son came to agree that teenagers in particular ought to be on a kind of sexual diet. Jimmy himself pointed out that a teen-aged boy, like anyone else, could get VD or could cause a girl to become pregnant. The father discussed the fact that sometimes sexual arousal can cause someone to be very much like a thirsty person who cannot find water, or a very hungry person who cannot find food.

In this particular conversation, Jimmy's father did not go into the view that Christian sexual intercourse is a part of a love commitment and that sex is more than simply a form of recreation. But by neither lecturing to his son nor trying to unload too much information and moral discourse on him in one or two sessions, Brad showed respect for him. Because Jimmy did not feel lectured to, the door was left open for more talks with his father on other days or weeks. The two of them did talk briefly about masturbation. Brad said that it was a much better alternative for teenage boys than their becoming involved sexually with someone. After assuring Jimmy that masturbation was quite wholesome and acceptable, Brad emphasized that excessive masturbation could become a nuisance if it should become something of a compulsion or addiction.

After further discussion of the matter, Brad and his son moved on eventually to another topic. The ground had been tilled, the seed planted, and the garden watered and cultivated. Brad had shown respect for his son's intelligence and moral sensitivity. And Jimmy in turn responded by showing respect for his father's concern that he be both a happy young person and morally responsible.

Being a parent is in a number of ways like being a farmer. Farmers cannot always predict exactly how their crops will grow. Hail storms, floods, pestilence, drought, and any number of unexpected threats might arise. However, farmers can pretty well predict that unless they and their fellow workers watch after the plants and care for them regularly, they most likely will either perish or do poorly. And so it is with our children. The unexpected will come to all families. In that sense, we can even learn to expect the unexpected—only we cannot always know what *form* it will take or *when* or *where* it will hit or whether it will be a pleasant surprise or a terrible shock. But like farmers, we parents must go about our work regularly, gently, and patiently. Different kinds of plants have to be treated differently, and our children must each be treated according to his or her unique personality. Earlier I quoted a passage from Paul that is applicable in the relationship between husband and wife. I wish to quote it again because it is so wonderfully applicable in the relationship between parents and children.

> *Brethren, if a man [or person] is overtaken in any trespass, you who are spiritual should restore him in a spirit of gentleness. Look to yourself, lest you too be tempted. Bear one another's burdens, and so fulfill the law of Christ. (Gal. 6:1-2 R.S.V.)*

Earlier in this chapter I noted that normally children of evangelical Christain parents do not always measure up to parental expectations. I tried to show that only in some cases is this a tragedy; in other cases it may be a very happy surprise. I wish now to turn to two other areas in which crises often come to the evangelical Christian married couple The middle-aged marriage seems to be a very unique and special phenomenon that has attracted the attention of noted students of marriage and the family. We must look at it in biblical perspective. Another phenomenon in marriage that may be either seriously disturbing or very rewarding is the change in job, career, or calling. I will close the chapter with a discussion of the job or career factor in the life of either husband or wife, or both of them.

The Middle-Aged Marriage—a Crisis

The Bible and Christian literature are filled with incidents of surprise and even shock in the marriages of believers. Imagine the reaction of Abraham and Sarah when they learned that at their very advanced age, and after years of childlessness, they would finally have a child. The Bible says that Abraham fell on his face and laughed at the news and that Sarah—apparently not as overtly emotional as Abraham—laughed to herself.

Some unexpected events are quite joyous. Sarah asked herself, " 'After I have grown old...shall I have pleasure?' " (Genesis 18:12 R.S.V.) It is not altogether clear whether she had in mind the pleasure of having sexual intercourse again with old Abraham or whether she was anticipating the pleasure of raising a son. Perhaps she was looking forward to both.

Unexpected events can sometimes lead to a depth and a healthy delight that the married couple had never before known during their entire relationship. The middle-aged marriage has often been described as the period of "marital blahs." "But," as one Christian marriage counselor noted, "for those couples who dare, the crisis of middle age can offer a chance to grow."[6]

It may sound strange to refer to the middle-aged period of marriage as a "crisis," but in many ways it is a serious crisis period. Indeed, this is the time when the marriage can begin to deteriorate rapidly. Decision by indecision is a common syndrome of this period. Often the middle-aged marriage may be compared to a ship drifting away from the shore and without anyone at the helm to steer it. Each spouse thinks that the marriage will simply take care of itself. To some extent, the other periods of marriage *have* crisis, whereas the middle-aged period *is* a crisis. Don and Lowrine had come to agree that their own marriage of seventeen years had died. Two individuals told me that the marriage had died of boredom. I do not know that this was in fact the case with Don and Lowrine, but we have all seen marriages die slowly of this dreadful malady. What is so strange in the case of Don and Lowrine is that neither seems to be boring to other people. They may have become boring only to one another.

Some Christian writers seem to want to ignore this fact of boredom in marriages. However, if a husband and wife can reconcile themselves to marital boredom, there may be no point in trying to change them, especially if each partner finds an interesting life in his or her work or in other avenues that are acceptable to Christian morality. Unfortunately, a boring marriage sometimes leads to depression for one or both partners. It is a depression that is usually born of the high expectation that the marriage be interesting and refreshing.

Donald Thomas, noted editor of *Successful Marriage*, thinks that it is during the stage of the "blahs" that married couples ought to take calculated risks in their marriage. What needs to be stressed, however, is that for many couples the middle-aged marriage is already dangerously risky. Boredom *is* a risk, and it is serious. I do not mean to say that it is the most dangerous condition to be in. But if by risk is meant a course of life that could lead to serious disturbance or even disaster, then boredom is indeed a dangerous risk. This is another way of saying that not even the placid marriage enjoys the guarantee that it will escape hitting on unexpected disasters. In fact, the middle-aged marriage has more than its share of divorces. For many couples, it is a time when marriage goes along placidly and then begins to fall apart without any way to recover a new balance.

For most middle-aged marriages the crisis lies in the fact that *the marriage simply cannot continue on the course that it has been going! Something has to change, whether for good or for ill.* Unfortunately, many Christians feel very guilty when they begin to sense this. They even feel that by looking favorably on any change at all, they are somehow being disloyal to their spouse and children.

The truth is that no one has complete control over his or her own life. Change is a part of *any* human relationship, and marriage is no exception. I have counseled with parents who could not face courageously the hard fact that their children had grown up and that the parent-child relationship had for them radically changed. And whether we like it or not, the marriage relationship simply takes new turns and twists over the years. Inasmuch as this is the case regardless sometimes of what we consciously do, a number of Christian specialists in marriage and family relations are beginning to advocate what may be called "creative change."

What this amounts to, to a great extent, is developing a new attitude toward change. Or to be more exact, it means getting clear as to what a marriage commitment really means or what marital faithfulness really is: *husband and wife are not married to their past, but instead are married to each other as changing human persons.* They are married to each other as individuals living in the *present,* not to some *memory* of what they used to be. He who would save his present marriage must lose his obsession with the past. Included in Christian faith is courage—courage to face the future with both its uncertainty and its challenging options. Indeed, there is no other alternative but to walk into the future, for the world is such that time is more than a mere illusion. Hindus may claim that time is unreal, but Christians are committed to the biblical view that time is a genuine category of human existence. And time is essentially *passage*—from past to present to future. People change, relationships change, and therefore marriages change, sometimes only gradually, at other times suddenly.

Followers of the Islamic religion have sometimes claimed that by taking on a second, third, or even fourth wife over a period of time, the man gains new experiences and relationships that enrich his life. In their concern to point out the disadvantages and hardships which accompany such polygamy, Christians have sometimes failed to admit there is a measure of truth in this Islamic claim. However, Christians may respond more positively that a monogamous marriage that is vital and sensitive has its own new experiences and development *within* marriage. Because time is a created reality and because change is a fact of life, no human being is "fixed" once and for all. At no point along the way can it be said that a person has finally "arrived" as a completed person. Therefore, each person is in some ways *a series of many "selves" coming into existence at different periods of time*. Hence, to live with one's wife or husband over a number of years is in a real sense to live with one person who is manifested as many emerging selves.

I cannot spell out here a complex theory of personhood. But I do wish to call attention to the position that because creation is still an ongoing process, each of us human beings is in process of being created anew. The fascinating thing about marriage is that a man and a woman have the opportunity of sharing in this challenging creative process, so that quite literally the husband helps to *create* the kind of being that his wife will become, and she in turn will share in the ongoing creation of her husband.

I must admit that my own wife has changed steadily (but not always predictably) over the years and that living with her has to some extent been like living with many women. There is more to this one woman than I had dreamed of over twenty years ago. It is a risky business—this marriage partnership. But with a proper attitude toward change and some careful planning, the risks can often prove worth all the uncertainty and hardship of marriage. If your spouse seems to be exactly the same person he or she was ten or thirty years ago, perhaps you need to look again at him or her. You have missed something—something very profound. Perhaps you need also to ask what you are doing to help your spouse's future "selves" to become responsible and happy, as well as interesting both to yourself and to himself or herself.

Literally speaking, the marriage commitment can take effect only in the present and in the future. Sometimes I ask myself, "I wonder what woman I will be married to five years from now?" I do not mean at all that my wife and I will have divorced by then, but rather that I expect that she will not be altogether the same woman by then that she is now. I am truly enjoying her as she is now, for that is what marriage is mostly about; but I am also keeping one eye on the future, since that is the only direction I have to travel in this marriage and in this life of transition. If human life has a certain "creative tension," this is partly because each individual is a pilgrim in transition. A remarkably successful marriage is two pilgrims who, while accepting the transitional dimension of all human life, have chosen to enrich the human process as best they can rather than simply suffer and endure it passively. However, not all marriages are remarkably successful and it is perhaps not fair to insist that they should be.

Beth and Luke

In a noted Christian college, Luke Stanley was looked up to by his classmates as a powerful young preacher. In his senior year he was elected as the first president of the Ministerial Association of the college. His fellow ministerial students agreed that here was a man destined to become either an extraordinary evangelist or an outstanding pastor of a large church. Luke, with his deep voice, stressed the evangelistic aspect of the Christian ministry. Having grown up in a Southern Baptist church, he had been taught that if he should preach faithfully the gospel, the Holy Spirit would surely reward his ministry by using him to lead large numbers of unbelievers to Christ. After graduating from seminary, Luke eagerly anticipated becoming a pastor and then receiving invitations from his fellow ministers to preach in revival meetings. He had prepared himself to go to work for the Lord, and now the time had come to do just that.

Over the next ten years, Luke discovered that the dreams and expectations about his ministry seemed never to be fulfilled.

Today, he is the pastor of a small congregation in a very small town. While many of his old classmates have much larger churches, Luke, still preaching faithfully the gospel, keeps wondering what has gone wrong. His ministerial friends know that for years he has been hoping to move on to "a better church." But he seems stuck where he has been for many years.

Quite naturally, Luke had entertained thoughts of being elected to serve as a major officer in his denomination—perhaps even president of the Baptist Convention of his state. But this was not to be. Indeed, his wife, Beth, a beautiful and talented woman, turned out to be the one destined to serve in influential positions at the state level. In college, no one would have predicted Beth's rise to important and responsible offices in her denomination, for she was always content to stand in the shadow of her husband-to-be. Today Beth has already served in the two highest offices that her state Baptist Convention has offered any woman. While Luke remains home in the small town to serve his small church, Beth flies here and there within and without the state to carry out efficiently her denominational responsibilities.

A few years ago, Luke, in his early forties, suffered an emotional or nervous breakdown. During all of his adult life, he had been preaching faithfully that Christ could and would solve deep personal problems if only people would open their hearts to him. Even those who knew Luke well could not feel the deep humiliation that overcame him when it seemed that the gospel that he preached had failed to work during his own personal crisis.

Every Christian could learn a great deal from Luke Stanley's case. It will help us to ask what went wrong. How could any minister of the gospel fall apart to the point that he had to leave his church for two months in order to receive special psychological help? Some of those who knew Luke best concluded that he very likely worried himself inordinately about whether he had some secret sin in his life, a sin which evoked God's displeasure and punishment. It is also possible that, without admitting it to himself, Luke gradually became angry with God. After all, like

Job, Luke had been an upright man who abhored evil. If anyone should claim that God was testing Luke, that person would have to admit that the test seems to have been terribly long, lasting over twenty years.

Before jumping to the conclusion that God selected this minister for a very special period of trial and testing, we would profit by looking at some unfortunate misconceptions that had influenced his behavior and state of mind. In the first place, Luke's own hometown minister and his friends at college and seminary had set him up for disillusionment when they strongly influenced him to believe that God always arranges to give a large church to dynamic preachers who faithfully preach especially the evangelistic aspect of the gospel. Sometimes Christian believers think that what they learn in church or from Christian leaders is always biblically sound teaching. Indeed, most of what they learn may be biblically sound, but the few unbiblical teachings that they absorb may become a source of great frustration and emotional harm to them. For example, it is true that in the Bible God promises that his word will not return to him void or empty (Isaiah 55:11). But this does not give any believer the right to presume that he or she knows exactly the channel through which God will work most effectively to bring his word back to him. In fact, Paul himself pointed out that while he planted the seed of the gospel and Apollos watered, it was God who eventually gave the growth (1 Cor. 3:6).

The second misconception that is often made by sincere Christian believers is that God calls some persons to be supermen and superwomen. Sometimes, in his sincere concern to win people to Christ, an evangelist will promise more than he has a right to promise on behalf of God. To claim to represent the thought of any other human being is a very serious matter. How much more serious is it to claim to represent God's thoughts on a variety of subjects. We often hear that the Christians must study the Scriptures in order not to be misguided by unbelievers. But what is often forgotten is that they need also to study the Scriptures in order not to be misguided by well-meaning Christians.

From a strictly biblical perspective, neither Luke nor any

other Christian has a right to expect to go through life without some major setbacks and crises. Success is a notoriously elusive and illusory ideal. Indeed, what does count as true success? Was Luke a failure because he never became the great evangelist or influential minister that people had expected him to be? Perhaps it would have helped Luke to see that what is success and failure in the eyes of people may not always be success and failure in God's eyes. The biblical view is that a person is successful in God's eyes if the person performs his or her calling faithfully.

But because Christians are only human, it is practically impossible for them to continue going on in life without some public manifestations of their faithfulness. After all, earth is not heaven. Indeed, in heaven rewards come freely and perpetually. On earth, rewards do not always come as expected. But the Christian cannot help desiring *some* rewards. This strong human desire must not be ridiculed, for Christians do not become superpersons upon becoming Christians. From birth to death, they remain finite human beings with the need to feel successful and rewarded in some of their undertakings.

One of the worst things we can teach our children is that they should never quit a task that they have begun. To teach them this is in effect to lead them to believe that they should disregard what experience can teach them. Only the person with a superperson complex could think that he or she should never give up on a project or even a career once it has begun. Luke Stanley, convinced that God had called him into the ministry, did not see clearly that the Christian ministry has many forms. The believer must not fall into the habit of thinking that God is as limited as he or she. It may very well be that Luke too quickly closed the door to other forms of the Christian ministry. Or it may be that God called him to be a pastor of a church for only ten years. I know of no biblical basis for assuming that when God calls a person into a very particular avenue of service, he does so for the rest of that person's life. Luke grew up in a setting in which he would have been called a quitter had he taken some other kind of vocation after having served as a pastor for ten or fifteen years. Indeed, he would have been regarded as someone who had gone back on his word, that is, had broken faith with God. Evangelical churches would do well to become more sensitive to the possibility that God can call one person to pursue more than one career or task in a lifetime.

Wives and husbands can be especially helpful to one another in dealing with a career that does not seem to be rewarding. Luke Stanley's father in particular would have been disappointed had Luke gone into another career. But Luke would be the first to insist that his father did not call him into the ministry in the first place. Of course, there are practical problems in changing careers. Luke, for example, is in his mid-forties, and it is very difficult to change professions at that age. Young men and women—and their parents—might learn from Luke Stanley's situation.

Beth Stanley feels a certain tension in her own life because of her work as an outstanding denominational leader. The question could be raised: should she resign her positions and stay home to give her husband emotional support in his frustrating situation? To answer yes without qualification is to forget that Beth has some claim to be rewarded by her work. Furthermore, could not the opportunity to serve her denomination be a divine calling for her, at least for a few years? Does God call only men to serve him outside the home? Given the way Luke was brought up, we can surmise that it was very disturbing for him to see his wife "succeed" at what he should have succeeded at, at least in his own mind and in that of his friends.

We rightly applaud Barnabas, who in some ways took second place to Paul in their work. But it may have taken far more grace and courage for Luke to support his wife Beth in her new calling than it did for Barnabas to support Paul. There is an old Christian hymn, "Take Time to Be Holy." We might wish for a hymn today entitled, "Take Time to Be Supportive," for indeed it literally does require considerable time for a husband and wife to give each other support and encouragement. No one ever fully knows what transpires between a husband

and wife in their private hours together, but we would profit by speculating about what, if we are married, our own marital relationship would be were we today in the situation of Luke and Beth Stanley. Life affords many surprising shifts and crises, so much so that the Christian husband and wife would do well to learn not to blame each other too quickly when things do not turn out as expected. It is well to expect our spouse to be responsible for certain tasks and roles in the marriage, otherwise the marriage will fall apart. But it is well also to know when to recognize that there are times when neither spouse has sufficient control over the variables. The Bible teaches that human beings are finite and that they do not have absolute strength to shape every part of their environment. Fortunate are the husband and wife who elect to enjoy the *process* of being married to one another rather than base their whole relationship on one finite goal that may never in this lifetime come into being, or at least not in the form in which they had expected.

I once knew a man who never did learn to enjoy each stage of the plants growing in his yard. For him, all that mattered was the "final" stage. Fortunately, down the street was another man who treated each stage of each tree and flower as something of a goal all its own. The second man received tenfold more pleasure and enjoyment from his plants. Similarly, the married couple that learns to cultivate new interests during each stage of their relationship will be ten-fold more interesting and rewarding to each other.

NOTES

Chapter 1 When Christians Become Depressed

[1]See Gerald F. Hawthorne (ed.), *Current Issues in Biblical and Patristic Interpretation* (Grand Rapids: Eerdmans, 1975).

[2]E. James Anthony and Therese Benedek (eds.), *Depression & Human Existence* (Boston: Little, Brown and Co., 1975), p. 536, note.

[3]O. Hobart Mowrer, *The Crisis in Psychiatry and Religion* (New York: D. Van Nostrand Co., 1961).

[4]Wayne E. Oates, *The Psychology of Religion* (Waco: Word Books, 1973), p. 179.

[5]Anthony and Benedek, p. 543.

[6]David L. Watson and Roland G. Tharp, *Self-Directed Behavior: Self-Modification for Personal Adjustment* (Monterey, California: Brooks/Cole Publishing Co., 1972), p. 48.

[7]See Karl R. Popper, *Conjectures and Refutations: The Growth of Scientific Knowledge* (New York: Harper Torchbooks, 1963), p. 67.

Chapter 2 When Christians Encounter Their Own Sexuality

[1]Herbert J. Miles, *Sexual Happiness in Marriage* (Grand Rapids: Zondervan Press, 1967).

[2]Dwight Hervey Small, *Christian: Celebrate Your Sexuality* (Old Tappan, N.J.: Fleming H. Revell Co., 1974), pp. 52, 165-167.

[3]Karl Menninger, *Whatever Became of Sin?* (New York: Hawthorn Books, Inc., 1973), pp. 31-37.

[4]Herbert J. Miles, *Sexual Understanding Before Marriage* (Grand Rapids: Zondervan, 1971), p. 150.

[5]See Norman Geisler, *Ethics: Alternatives and Issues* (Grand Rapids: Zondervan, 1971), pp. 200-201.

Chapter 3 When Christians Face the Question of Abortion

[1]R.F.R. Gardner, *Abortion: The Personal Dilemma*, revised American edition (Old Tappan, N.J.: Fleming H. Revell Co., Spire Books, 1974), p. 286. Originally published by Paternoster Press in 1972.

[2]José M.R. Delgado, *Physical Control of the Mind: Toward a Psychocivilized Society* (New York: Harper & Row, 1969), p. 44.

[3]*Ibid.*, p. 45.

[4]*Ibid.*

[5]*Ibid.*, p. 48

[6]*Ibid.*

[7]*Ibid.*, p. 49.

[8]See Peter Nathan, *The Nervous System* (Philadelphia: J.B. Lippincott Co., 1969), p. 163.

[9]See J.A. Loraine and E.T. Bell, *Fertility and Contraception in the Human Female* (Edinburgh: Livingston Press, 1968).

[10]Vincent C. Punzo, *Reflective Naturalism: An Introduction to Moral Philosophy* (New York: Macmillan Co., 1969), p. 212.

[11]See Edgar Young Mullins, *The Christian Religion in Its Doctrinal Expression* (Philadelphia: Judson Press, 1917), pp. 262-264.

[12]J. Stafford Wright, "Traducianism," in *Baker's Dictionary of Theology,* Everett F. Harrison, ed. (Grand Rapids: Baker Book House, 1960), p. 527.

[13]Mullins, p. 263.

[14]Wright, p. 527.

[15]See Mullins, p. 257; Mark G. Cambron, *Bible Doctrines: Beliefs That Matter* (Grand Rapids: Zondervan, 1954), p. 158.

[16]See Cambron, p. 158.

[17]See Richard Quebedeaux, *The Young Evangelicals* (New York: Harper & Row, 1974), p. 82.

[18]Gardner, p. 315, quoting from Daniel Callahan, *Abortion: Law, Choice and Morality* (New York: Macmillan, 1970).

Chapter 4 When Christians Divorce

[1]B. David Edens, "The Fine Line of Successful Marriage," *Baptist and Reflector*, 140:43 (October 24, 1974), 15.

[2]*Baptist and Reflector*, 140:39 (Sept. 26, 1974), 3. See also *Baptist and Reflector,* 140:32 (August 8, 1974), 15; *Baptist and Reflector,* 140:31 (August 1, 1974), 9; *Baptist and Reflector,* 40:6 (Feb. 7, 1974), 15.

[3]David Edens, "Living in a Divorced Society," *Baptist and Reflector*, 140:32 (August 8, 1974), 15.

[4]See Roland Bainton, *Here I Stand: A Life of Martin Luther* (New York: Mentor Books, 1950), p. 293.

[5]See William Graham Cole, *Sex in Christianity and Psychoanalysis* (New York: Oxford University Press, 1955), pp. 116-118.

[6]See T.W. Manson, *The Teaching of Jesus*, second edition (New York: Cambridge University Press, 1935), p. 292 note 5; C.E.P. Cox, *The Gospel According to Saint Matthew* (London: SCM Press, 1952), pp. 122f.

[7]Basil F.C. Atkinson, "Commentary," in F. Davidson, ed., *The New Bible Commentary*, second edition (Grand Rapids: Eerdmans, 1954), p. 780.

[8]*Ibid.*, italics added.

[9]*Ibid.*, italics added.

[10]B. Harvie Branscomb, *The Teachings of Jesus* (New York: Abingdon Press, 1931), p. 244.

Chapter 5 Marriage and the Weakness of the Flesh

[1]Dan Greenburg, *How to Be a Jewish Mother* (New York: The New American Library, Inc., Signet Books, 1965), p. 15.

[2]Cort R. Flint, ed., *The Quotable Billy Graham* (Anderson, S.C.: Drake House, 1966), p. 81, italics added.

[3]*Ibid.*

[4]Robert Lindner, *The Fifty-Minute Hour* (New York: Bantam Books, 1971), p. 70.

[5]See also Michael J. Mahoney and Kathryn Mahoney, "Fight Fat with Behavior Control," *Psychology Today*, 9:12 (May 1976), 39-43, 92-94. Mahoney and Mahoney, *Permanent Weight Control* (New York: Norton, 1976).

Chapter 6 Marital Openness Through Creative Listening

[1]See Charles Thraux, "Reinforcement and Nonreinforcement in Rogerian Psychotherapy," *Journal of Abnormal Psychology,* 71:1 (1966), 1-9.

[2]See William Lederer and Don Jackson, *The Mirages of Marriage* (New York: Norton, 1968).

[3]*Ibid.*, p. 177.

Chapter 7 The Greatest of These Is Love

[1]Victor Raimy, *Misunderstanding of the Self: Cognitive Psychotherapy and the Misconception Hypothesis* (San Francisco: Jossey-Bass Inc., 1975), p. 124. Raimy is quoting Adler in H.L. and R.R. Ansbacher, eds., *The Individual Psychology of Alfred Adler* (New York: Harper & Row, 1956), p. 343.

[2]Raimy, p. 159.

[3]Under certain extreme conditions a person might act and behave in such a way as to raise seriously the question as to whether he or she has in fact become *another person*. But this is a highly complex issue which cannot be pursued in this book.

[4]See Bruce Larson, *Ask Me to Dance* (Waco: Word Books, 1972), p. 97.

Chapter 8 The Myth of the Complete Person

[1]Cole, p. 7.

[2]Marabel Morgan, *The Total Woman* (Old Tappan, N.J.: Fleming H. Revell, 1973).

[3]This quotation is taken from Hinkle's address delivered at the Glorieta Baptist Conference Center and is recorded in Mike Chute's report "Good Marriages Obtainable, Not Given," *Baptist and Reflector*, 141:44 (Oct. 30, 1975), 9.

[4]Some New Testament commentators contend that Jesus was talking of "maturity" rather than "perfection." But Jesus' humor still holds, for any serious comparison between God and humankind on this criterion would also have been so absurd as to evoke at least a smile. My interpretation of this passage fits with the Reformation view that the law's primary function is to show men and women that they are indeed so incomplete as to be in need of grace.

[5]Max Weber, *The Protestant Ethic and the Spirit of Capitalism*, trans. Talcott Parsons (New York: Charles Scribner's Sons, 1956).

[6]Wayne Oates, *Confessions of a Workaholic* (Nashville: Abingdon Press, 1971).

[7]See Margaret Movius, "Voluntary Childlessness," *The Family Coordinator*, 25:1 (January 1976), 57-63.

[8]James O'Toole, "The American Future: The Reserve Army of the Underemployed: I—The World of Work," *Change*, 7:4 (May 1975), 32.

Chapter 9 Dealing with the Unexpected

[1]Quoted in *Baptist and Reflector*, 142:15 (April 8, 1976), 4.

[2]Edward John Carnell, *The Kingdom of Love and the Pride of Life* (Grand Rapids: Eerdmans, 1960), p. 117.

[3]*Baptist and Reflector*, 142:11 (March 11, 1976).

[4]See Robert G. Torbet, *A History of the Baptists* (Philadelphia: Judson Press, 1950), p. 77.

[5]Carnell, *Christian Commitment* (New York: Macmillan, 1957), p. 199.

[6]B. David Edens, "Middle-Aged Marriage," *Baptist and Reflector*, 142:3 (January 15, 1976), 15.